MASTERING ALGORITHMS WITH C++

Advanced Algorithms Explained

THOMPSON CARTER

TABLE OF CONTENTS

Introduction

Mastering Algorithms with C++: Advanced Algorithms Explained

In the ever-evolving world of computer science, algorithms serve as the fundamental building blocks of problem-solving. Whether you're designing software, developing games, analyzing data, or optimizing systems, the efficiency of your algorithms determines the performance, scalability, and success of your solution. As the problems we tackle become increasingly complex, mastering advanced algorithms is essential to pushing the boundaries of what's possible in computing.

This book, ***Mastering Algorithms with C++: Advanced Algorithms Explained***, is designed for programmers who want to go beyond basic algorithm knowledge and dive deep into the advanced techniques that power today's most cutting-edge applications. Written with clarity and accessibility in mind, this guide offers jargon-free explanations, hands-on examples, and real-world case studies that will help you understand and implement algorithms with confidence, while leveraging the power of C++ for optimal performance.

Why Algorithms and Why C++?

Algorithms are the heart and soul of programming. From simple tasks like sorting data to complex computations like machine learning and optimization, algorithms determine how efficiently we can solve problems. But it's not enough to understand the theory behind algorithms; you must also be equipped to implement them effectively and choose the right algorithm for a given problem.

C++ is a perfect language for studying and implementing algorithms. As one of the most powerful and widely used programming languages, C++ offers both **high-level abstractions** and **low-level control**, making it ideal for both learning and performance. Its ability to efficiently manage memory, control hardware, and handle complex computations ensures that algorithms run quickly and reliably—qualities essential when working with advanced algorithms, where execution speed and memory usage are critical.

What You Will Learn

This book will take you on a journey through a wide variety of **advanced algorithms**, covering both **theory** and **practical implementation** in C++. With each chapter, you'll gain a deeper understanding of the key concepts behind these algorithms and the real-world problems they solve.

Here's an overview of what you'll explore:

1. **Foundations of Algorithms**: Before we delve into more complex topics, we'll lay the groundwork by revisiting basic concepts such as algorithm complexity, time and space tradeoffs, and why algorithm selection matters. You'll understand how to evaluate and compare algorithms to make informed decisions about which to use for your projects.

2. **Advanced Techniques and Approaches**: As we progress, you'll learn about the more intricate techniques that solve advanced problems, such as **dynamic programming**, **greedy algorithms**, **backtracking**, **graph algorithms**, and **network flow algorithms**. We'll walk you through how these algorithms work, when to use them, and how to implement them efficiently in C++.

3. **Algorithm Optimization**: We'll dive into techniques for optimizing algorithms, improving performance, and solving problems in less time and with fewer resources. You'll learn how to analyze the performance of your code and understand how different algorithms and data structures interact to provide the most efficient solution.

4. **Graph and Network Algorithms**: In the real world, many problems are best represented as **graphs**—from social networks to transportation systems, communication networks, and more. We'll study graph algorithms like **Dijkstra's algorithm**, **Bellman-Ford**, and **minimum**

spanning trees, along with techniques for solving problems such as **shortest path**, **flow networks**, and **graph traversal**.

5. **Specialized Algorithms**: Throughout the book, we'll also explore more specialized algorithms, such as **string matching algorithms**, **computational geometry algorithms**, and **randomized algorithms**. These topics have broad applications, from text searching to geographic data analysis, and will enhance your ability to solve a diverse range of problems.

6. **Machine Learning Algorithms**: Finally, we'll delve into the algorithms that power machine learning. We'll study classic algorithms like **linear regression**, **decision trees**, and **k-means clustering**, and demonstrate how to implement them in C++ to solve real-world machine learning tasks.

Real-World Applications

This book focuses not only on algorithm theory but also on **real-world applications**. Each chapter includes practical examples that illustrate how the algorithms discussed can be used to solve common problems in software development, data analysis, optimization, and machine learning.

For example, we'll explore how **graph algorithms** are used to build efficient routing systems in **GPS navigation** or how **dynamic programming** can solve optimization problems in fields like **resource management** and **finance**. We'll also look at how **machine learning algorithms** can be applied to tasks like **predictive analytics**, **image recognition**, and **natural language processing**.

Through these examples, you'll see how the algorithms in this book are not just theoretical constructs, but powerful tools that drive real-world innovation and problem-solving.

Why This Book?

Whether you are a seasoned developer or an aspiring computer scientist, mastering advanced algorithms will set you apart as a problem solver. This book is designed for those who want to deepen their understanding of algorithms and elevate their programming skills. By combining in-depth theory with practical implementation in C++, we aim to equip you with the knowledge and tools you need to tackle even the most complex algorithmic challenges.

Here are some of the key benefits of this book:

- **Clear Explanations**: Concepts are explained in simple, jargon-free language, with each algorithm broken down step-by-step.

- **Hands-On C++ Code**: Each chapter contains real-world examples implemented in C++, so you can see how the theory translates into practical code.

- **Optimized Algorithms**: Emphasis is placed on algorithm optimization, ensuring that you understand how to choose the most efficient algorithm for your task.

- **Real-World Use Cases**: Through practical examples, you'll gain insights into how these algorithms are used in industries like software development, AI, data science, and more.

- **Comprehensive Coverage**: From basic algorithmic techniques to cutting-edge topics in machine learning and quantum computing, this book covers a broad range of advanced topics in algorithm design.

Mastering Algorithms with C++: Advanced Algorithms Explained is more than just a book on algorithms—it's a comprehensive guide to solving real-world problems through algorithmic thinking. Whether you're looking to optimize your code, tackle more complex challenges, or prepare for interviews that require advanced algorithm knowledge, this book will provide you with the tools, examples, and insights you need to succeed.

As you work through this book, you'll not only gain a deeper understanding of algorithms but also develop the problem-solving mindset necessary to approach complex challenges in programming. With C++ as your tool of choice, you'll be well-equipped to implement efficient and scalable solutions that can handle today's computational demands and beyond.

Chapter 1: Introduction to Algorithms and C++

What Are Algorithms?

At its core, an **algorithm** is a well-defined, step-by-step procedure or set of rules for solving a problem or achieving a specific task. Algorithms are the backbone of computer science, and they play a crucial role in solving problems efficiently. They can range from simple procedures like adding two numbers to more complex ones such as sorting large datasets, optimizing network routes, or even training machine learning models.

An algorithm typically has the following characteristics:

1. **Input**: The algorithm takes some input values or data.
2. **Output**: After processing the input, it generates an output.
3. **Finiteness**: The algorithm must terminate after a finite number of steps.
4. **Definiteness**: Each step must be precisely defined.
5. **Effectiveness**: The steps must be simple enough to be carried out, in theory, with basic resources.

Common examples of algorithms include:

- **Sorting algorithms** (e.g., QuickSort, MergeSort).
- **Searching algorithms** (e.g., Binary Search).

- **Graph algorithms** (e.g., Dijkstra's algorithm).
- **Mathematical algorithms** (e.g., Euclidean algorithm for finding the greatest common divisor).

Why C++ for Algorithm Implementation?

C++ is widely considered one of the best languages for implementing algorithms for several reasons:

1. **Performance**: C++ is a compiled language known for its high performance. Unlike interpreted languages (like Python), C++ code is compiled directly to machine code, which can make it run faster—especially important when working with large datasets or computationally intensive tasks.

2. **Control Over Resources**: C++ provides detailed control over system resources (like memory and CPU), which is crucial for optimizing algorithm efficiency. This fine-grained control makes C++ ideal for implementing complex algorithms that need to be highly optimized for speed and memory usage.

3. **Data Structures**: C++ has built-in support for powerful data structures (arrays, linked lists, stacks, queues, hash tables, etc.) that are essential for implementing various algorithms. Additionally, the **Standard Template Library (STL)** provides pre-built templates for many commonly used data structures, such as vectors, maps, and sets,

making it easier to focus on algorithm design rather than data structure implementation.

4. **Object-Oriented Programming (OOP)**: C++ supports object-oriented programming, allowing you to structure your algorithm-based solutions in a modular and reusable way. This is useful for large-scale projects where multiple algorithms and data structures interact.

5. **Portability**: C++ code is portable across different platforms and systems, which makes it easy to test and deploy algorithms on various devices and environments.

While C++ may not be as easy to learn as some other languages, its efficiency, control, and scalability make it an excellent choice for algorithmic development, especially when performance matters.

Understanding Algorithm Complexity (Time and Space Complexity)

When implementing algorithms, it's crucial to understand their **complexity**. This helps you assess how well the algorithm will perform as the size of the input grows. There are two main types of complexity to consider:

1. **Time Complexity**:
    o Time complexity refers to how the runtime of an algorithm increases as the size of the input data increases.

o It is usually expressed using **Big O notation**, which provides an upper bound on the number of operations an algorithm will perform in the worst-case scenario.

o For example:

  ▪ A simple **linear search** has a time complexity of **O(n)**, meaning the time it takes grows linearly with the size of the input list.

  ▪ **MergeSort**, on the other hand, has a time complexity of **O(n log n)**, meaning its runtime increases more slowly as the input size grows.

Common time complexities you'll encounter:

o **O(1)**: Constant time, regardless of input size (e.g., accessing an element in an array).

o **O(log n)**: Logarithmic time (e.g., binary search).

o **O(n)**: Linear time (e.g., linear search).

o **O(n log n)**: Log-linear time (e.g., merge sort, quicksort).

o **O(n²)**: Quadratic time (e.g., bubble sort).

2. **Space Complexity**:

o Space complexity refers to the amount of memory or space an algorithm needs to run relative to the input size.

o Like time complexity, space complexity is also expressed in **Big O notation**.

o For example, if an algorithm requires a fixed amount of space for any input size, its space complexity is **O(1)**. If the space required grows linearly with the input size, the space complexity is **O(n)**.

Common space complexities include:

o **O(1)**: Constant space (e.g., algorithms that don't use any extra memory aside from variables).

o **O(n)**: Linear space (e.g., storing a list of input elements).

Real-World Example: Choosing the Right Algorithm for a Problem

Imagine you are tasked with building an application that sorts a list of customer orders based on the order date. The list can range from a few dozen to millions of records. To choose the right algorithm, you need to consider:

• **Small Data Set**: If the number of records is small (e.g., less than 100), a simple algorithm like **Bubble Sort** ($O(n^2)$)

could suffice, even though it is inefficient for larger datasets.

- **Large Data Set**: If the number of records is large, more efficient algorithms like **MergeSort** (O(n log n)) or **QuickSort** (O(n log n) average, O(n²) worst case) would be better because they scale much better with larger datasets.

Additionally, if you need the application to be highly responsive, you might choose an **in-place sorting algorithm** like **QuickSort**, which uses very little extra space. If stability is important (i.e., records with the same order date should appear in the same order as they were input), then **MergeSort** would be a better choice since it is stable.

In this chapter, we covered the foundational concepts of algorithms and their implementation in C++. We discussed:

- The importance of algorithms and their role in problem-solving.
- Why C++ is an excellent language for implementing algorithms, thanks to its efficiency, control over resources, and rich set of data structures.
- The basics of algorithm complexity, including time and space complexity, and how to evaluate algorithms based on their performance.

- A real-world example of how to choose the right algorithm for sorting a list of customer orders.

In the following chapters, we will dive deeper into specific algorithms, exploring their intricacies, performance, and implementation in C++, with real-world examples and applications.

Chapter 2: Recursion and Divide-and-Conquer Algorithms

Introduction to Recursion: How It Works

Recursion is a fundamental concept in computer science where a function calls itself in order to solve a problem. In other words, a recursive function solves a smaller instance of the same problem until it reaches a simple case, known as the **base case**, which can be solved directly. After the base case is reached, the function works its way back up, combining the results to solve the original problem.

In simpler terms, recursion breaks a problem down into smaller subproblems that are easier to manage, solves those subproblems by calling the same function, and then combines the results of these smaller subproblems to arrive at the final solution.

A basic recursive function has two main parts:

1. **Base Case**: This is the condition where the function stops calling itself. It's typically the simplest case of the problem.
2. **Recursive Case**: This is where the function calls itself with modified arguments to solve a smaller subproblem.

A classic example of recursion is calculating the **factorial** of a number. The factorial of n (denoted as n!) is the product of all positive integers less than or equal to n, and it can be defined recursively:

- **Factorial Function**:
    - $n! = n \times (n-1)!$ (for $n > 0$)
    - $0! = 1$ (base case)

cpp

```
int factorial(int n) {
   if (n == 0) {
     return 1;  // Base case
   } else {
     return n * factorial(n - 1);  // Recursive case
   }
}
```

In this example, the function calls itself until it reaches the base case where n == 0, and then it starts returning values as it "unwinds" the recursion.

While recursion is powerful, it can also be inefficient for certain types of problems due to repeated calculations and excessive use of stack memory. To mitigate these issues, understanding the principles behind recursion and recognizing when iterative solutions may be more efficient is key.

Basic Divide-and-Conquer Algorithms

Divide-and-conquer is a design paradigm based on recursion. The core idea behind divide-and-conquer is to break a large problem down into smaller subproblems, solve the subproblems independently (often recursively), and then combine the results of the subproblems to get the final solution. This approach is used to design efficient algorithms, particularly when the problem can be divided into similar subproblems.

The divide-and-conquer strategy typically involves three steps:

1. **Divide**: Break the problem into smaller, more manageable subproblems.
2. **Conquer**: Recursively solve each of the subproblems.
3. **Combine**: Merge the results of the subproblems into a final solution.

Some well-known divide-and-conquer algorithms include:

- **Merge Sort**: A sorting algorithm that splits the list into halves, recursively sorts them, and merges the sorted halves.
- **QuickSort**: A sorting algorithm that divides the array into two subarrays based on a pivot element and recursively sorts each subarray.
- **Binary Search**: A searching algorithm that divides the search interval in half and recursively searches one of the halves.

Real-World Example: Solving a Problem Using Recursion (e.g., Merge Sort, QuickSort)

Let's take a deeper look at two classic **divide-and-conquer** algorithms: **Merge Sort** and **QuickSort**, which are both based on recursion.

Merge Sort

Merge Sort is a **recursive sorting algorithm** that follows the divide-and-conquer paradigm. The array is recursively divided into halves until each subarray has only one element (base case). Then, the subarrays are merged back together in sorted order.

Here's how Merge Sort works:

1. **Divide**: Split the array into two halves.
2. **Conquer**: Recursively sort the two halves.
3. **Combine**: Merge the sorted halves back together.

cpp

```cpp
#include <iostream>
#include <vector>
using namespace std;

// Merge function that combines two sorted subarrays into one sorted array
void merge(vector<int>& arr, int left, int mid, int right) {
    int n1 = mid - left + 1;
    int n2 = right - mid;
```

```cpp
vector<int> leftArr(n1), rightArr(n2);

for (int i = 0; i < n1; i++)
    leftArr[i] = arr[left + i];
for (int j = 0; j < n2; j++)
    rightArr[j] = arr[mid + 1 + j];

int i = 0, j = 0, k = left;
while (i < n1 && j < n2) {
    if (leftArr[i] <= rightArr[j]) {
        arr[k] = leftArr[i];
        i++;
    } else {
        arr[k] = rightArr[j];
        j++;
    }
    k++;
}

while (i < n1) {
    arr[k] = leftArr[i];
    i++;
    k++;
}

while (j < n2) {
    arr[k] = rightArr[j];
    j++;
    k++;
}
```

```
}


// MergeSort function that recursively divides and sorts the array
void mergeSort(vector<int>& arr, int left, int right) {
    if (left >= right)
        return;
    int mid = left + (right - left) / 2;
    mergeSort(arr, left, mid);  // Recursively sort the left half
    mergeSort(arr, mid + 1, right);  // Recursively sort the right half
    merge(arr, left, mid, right);  // Merge the two sorted halves
}


int main() {
    vector<int> arr = {12, 11, 13, 5, 6, 7};
    int n = arr.size();
    mergeSort(arr, 0, n - 1);

    cout << "Sorted array: ";
    for (int i : arr) {
        cout << i << " ";
    }
    return 0;
}
```

In the code above, the mergeSort function divides the array into two halves, recursively sorts each half, and then merges the sorted halves using the merge function.

QuickSort

QuickSort is another **recursive sorting algorithm** that works by selecting a pivot element and partitioning the array into two subarrays: one with elements smaller than the pivot and one with elements greater than the pivot. The subarrays are then sorted recursively.

Here's how QuickSort works:

1. **Divide**: Pick a pivot element and partition the array into two subarrays.
2. **Conquer**: Recursively sort the two subarrays.
3. **Combine**: The array is already sorted after the recursive steps.

cpp

```cpp
#include <iostream>
#include <vector>
using namespace std;

// Partition function that rearranges elements based on the pivot
int partition(vector<int>& arr, int low, int high) {
    int pivot = arr[high];
    int i = (low - 1);

    for (int j = low; j <= high - 1; j++) {
        if (arr[j] < pivot) {
            i++;
            swap(arr[i], arr[j]);
        }
    }
}
```

```
    swap(arr[i + 1], arr[high]);
    return (i + 1);
}


// QuickSort function that recursively sorts the array
void quickSort(vector<int>& arr, int low, int high) {
    if (low < high) {
        int pi = partition(arr, low, high);  // Partitioning index
        quickSort(arr, low, pi - 1);  // Recursively sort the left subarray
        quickSort(arr, pi + 1, high);  // Recursively sort the right subarray
    }
}

int main() {
    vector<int> arr = {10, 7, 8, 9, 1, 5};
    int n = arr.size();
    quickSort(arr, 0, n - 1);

    cout << "Sorted array: ";
    for (int i : arr) {
        cout << i << " ";
    }
    return 0;
}
```

In the code above, the quickSort function selects a pivot and partitions the array into two subarrays, recursively sorting each subarray.

In this chapter, we introduced the concept of **recursion** and how it forms the foundation of **divide-and-conquer algorithms**. We covered:

- The mechanics of recursion and how it works through self-calls and base cases.
- How divide-and-conquer strategies break down complex problems into smaller subproblems, making them easier to solve.
- Real-world examples like **Merge Sort** and **QuickSort**, demonstrating how recursion and divide-and-conquer are used to efficiently sort arrays.

In the next chapter, we will explore additional advanced algorithmic concepts and their practical applications in C++.

Chapter 3: Sorting Algorithms

Sorting is a fundamental concept in computer science. Sorting algorithms are essential for efficiently organizing data in a specific order—whether in ascending or descending order. The choice of sorting algorithm can drastically impact the performance of your program, especially when dealing with large datasets. In this chapter, we'll explore several popular sorting algorithms, including **Bubble Sort**, **Selection Sort**, and **Insertion Sort**, and analyze their strengths, weaknesses, and real-world applications.

Understanding Sorting Algorithms and Their Use Cases

Sorting is a crucial operation used in a wide variety of applications, such as searching, organizing data, optimizing other algorithms (e.g., binary search), and simplifying problems like finding the median or mode. Sorting algorithms come in various types, each with different performance characteristics. They can be classified based on:

- **Time Complexity**: How the running time increases as the size of the dataset grows.
- **Space Complexity**: How much extra memory the algorithm requires.
- **Stability**: Whether or not the algorithm preserves the relative order of elements with equal values.

- **Adaptiveness**: Whether the algorithm performs better on partially sorted data.

While there are several advanced sorting algorithms such as **QuickSort**, **Merge Sort**, and **Heap Sort**, this chapter focuses on **comparison-based algorithms** with simple implementations: **Bubble Sort**, **Selection Sort**, and **Insertion Sort**.

Each of these algorithms is useful in specific situations based on the problem's constraints, such as small datasets, simplicity of implementation, or when memory usage is a critical factor.

In-Depth Analysis of Bubble Sort, Selection Sort, and Insertion Sort

1. Bubble Sort

Bubble Sort is one of the simplest sorting algorithms, but also one of the least efficient. It works by repeatedly stepping through the list, comparing adjacent elements, and swapping them if they are in the wrong order. This process is repeated until the list is sorted.

How it works:

- Start at the beginning of the list.
- Compare each pair of adjacent elements.
- If the elements are out of order, swap them.

- Continue this process through the entire list, each time ignoring the last sorted element (since it's in its correct position).
- Repeat until no more swaps are needed.

Time Complexity:

- **Worst-case**: $O(n^2)$
- **Best-case**: $O(n)$ (when the list is already sorted, but the algorithm still checks all pairs)
- **Average-case**: $O(n^2)$

Space Complexity: $O(1)$, as Bubble Sort is an **in-place** algorithm (it doesn't require additional memory beyond the input list).

When to use: Bubble Sort is rarely used in practice due to its inefficiency for large datasets, but it's a good introductory algorithm to learn about sorting principles.

Example (Bubble Sort):

cpp

```
#include <iostream>
#include <vector>
using namespace std;

void bubbleSort(vector<int>& arr) {
    int n = arr.size();
```

```
   bool swapped;
  for (int i = 0; i < n-1; i++) {
     swapped = false;
     for (int j = 0; j < n-i-1; j++) {
       if (arr[j] > arr[j+1]) {
          swap(arr[j], arr[j+1]);
          swapped = true;
       }
     }
     // If no two elements were swapped, the list is already sorted
     if (!swapped) {
        break;
     }
  }
}

int main() {
  vector<int> arr = {5, 1, 4, 2, 8};
  bubbleSort(arr);
  for (int i : arr) {
     cout << i << " ";
  }
  return 0;
}
```

2. Selection Sort

Selection Sort is another simple sorting algorithm that works by repeatedly finding the minimum element from the unsorted part of the list and swapping it with the first unsorted element. This process continues until the list is sorted.

How it works:

- Start with the first element.
- Find the minimum element in the unsorted part of the list.
- Swap it with the first unsorted element.
- Move to the next element and repeat the process until the list is sorted.

Time Complexity:

- **Worst-case**: $O(n^2)$
- **Best-case**: $O(n^2)$
- **Average-case**: $O(n^2)$

Space Complexity: $O(1)$, as Selection Sort is also an **in-place** algorithm.

When to use: Selection Sort is more efficient than Bubble Sort in some cases, especially when minimizing swaps is important (though it still has a quadratic time complexity). It's not suitable for large datasets.

Example (Selection Sort):

cpp

```
#include <iostream>
#include <vector>
using namespace std;
```

```cpp
void selectionSort(vector<int>& arr) {
    int n = arr.size();
    for (int i = 0; i < n-1; i++) {
        int minIndex = i;
        for (int j = i+1; j < n; j++) {
            if (arr[j] < arr[minIndex]) {
                minIndex = j;
            }
        }
        swap(arr[i], arr[minIndex]);
    }
}

int main() {
    vector<int> arr = {29, 10, 14, 37, 13};
    selectionSort(arr);
    for (int i : arr) {
        cout << i << " ";
    }
    return 0;
}
```

3. Insertion Sort

Insertion Sort builds the final sorted array one item at a time by taking each element from the unsorted part and inserting it into its correct position in the sorted part.

How it works:

- Start with the second element (the first element is trivially sorted).
- Compare it with the elements in the sorted part of the list and insert it in the correct position.
- Repeat this process for all elements.

Time Complexity:

- **Worst-case**: $O(n^2)$
- **Best-case**: $O(n)$ (when the list is already sorted)
- **Average-case**: $O(n^2)$

Space Complexity: $O(1)$, as Insertion Sort is also an **in-place** algorithm.

When to use: Insertion Sort is efficient for small datasets or nearly sorted data, and it's often used in practice for small subarrays within more complex algorithms.

Example (Insertion Sort):

cpp

```cpp
#include <iostream>
#include <vector>
using namespace std;

void insertionSort(vector<int>& arr) {
    int n = arr.size();
```

```cpp
for (int i = 1; i < n; i++) {
    int key = arr[i];
    int j = i - 1;
    // Move elements of arr[0..i-1] that are greater than key
    // to one position ahead of their current position
    while (j >= 0 && arr[j] > key) {
        arr[j + 1] = arr[j];
        j = j - 1;
    }
    arr[j + 1] = key;
  }
}

int main() {
    vector<int> arr = {12, 11, 13, 5, 6};
    insertionSort(arr);
    for (int i : arr) {
        cout << i << " ";
    }
    return 0;
}
```

Real-World Example: Choosing the Right Sorting Algorithm Based on Data Type and Size

When deciding which sorting algorithm to use, it's important to consider the following factors:

1. **Data Size**:
   - o For **small datasets** (a few hundred elements), simple algorithms like **Bubble Sort, Selection Sort,**

or **Insertion Sort** can work fine due to their straightforward implementation.

- o For **large datasets**, more advanced sorting algorithms such as **QuickSort** or **Merge Sort** should be used, as they have much better performance (O(n log n)).

2. **Data Characteristics**:

- o If the data is already **almost sorted**, **Insertion Sort** can be a good choice because its best-case time complexity is O(n), making it very efficient when the list is nearly sorted.
- o If the data is **random**, **QuickSort** or **Merge Sort** are more efficient due to their O(n log n) time complexity.

3. **Memory Constraints**:

- o **Selection Sort**, **Bubble Sort**, and **Insertion Sort** are all **in-place** algorithms that require constant memory, so they can be useful when memory is limited.
- o **Merge Sort**, although efficient, requires additional memory (O(n)) for the merging process, making it less suitable for memory-constrained environments.

In this chapter, we covered the basics of **Bubble Sort, Selection Sort**, and **Insertion Sort**, three fundamental but inefficient sorting algorithms. These algorithms are easy to implement but have quadratic time complexity, making them unsuitable for large datasets.

- **Bubble Sort** is the simplest but least efficient.
- **Selection Sort** minimizes swaps but still has quadratic time complexity.
- **Insertion Sort** is efficient for small or nearly sorted datasets but still performs poorly on large, unsorted datasets.

In the next chapter, we'll explore more efficient sorting algorithms and discuss how to implement them in C++ for larger datasets.

Chapter 4: Binary Search and Search Algorithms

In this chapter, we'll delve into **search algorithms**, focusing on **Binary Search**—one of the most efficient searching techniques for **sorted data**. We'll explore different types of search algorithms, how they operate, and their real-world applications. Additionally, we'll examine how searching in **sorted** vs **unsorted** data impacts algorithm performance, and we'll wrap up with a real-world example of implementing **Binary Search** for a database query.

Binary Search and Its Variations

Binary Search is a classic searching algorithm that efficiently locates an element in a sorted dataset. It operates by repeatedly dividing the search interval in half and determining which half of the list may contain the target value, based on a comparison. The algorithm continues to narrow down the search space until the target element is found or the search space is empty.

How Binary Search Works:

1. Start with the middle element of the sorted list.
2. If the middle element is the target value, return the index.
3. If the target value is smaller than the middle element, narrow the search to the left half of the list.

4. If the target value is larger than the middle element, narrow the search to the right half of the list.

5. Repeat this process until the target is found or the search space is empty.

Time Complexity:

- **Worst-case**: O(log n), because the search space is halved with each iteration.
- **Best-case**: O(1), if the middle element is the target.
- **Average-case**: O(log n).

Space Complexity: O(1), because Binary Search is an **in-place** algorithm that does not require extra memory for additional data structures.

Example (Binary Search):

cpp

```
#include <iostream>
#include <vector>
using namespace std;

int binarySearch(const vector<int>& arr, int target) {
    int left = 0, right = arr.size() - 1;

    while (left <= right) {
        int mid = left + (right - left) / 2;
```

```
    // Check if the target is present at mid
    if (arr[mid] == target) {
        return mid; // Target found
    }

    // If target is smaller, ignore right half
    if (arr[mid] > target) {
        right = mid - 1;
    }
    // If target is larger, ignore left half
    else {
        left = mid + 1;
    }
    }
    return -1; // Target not found
}

int main() {
    vector<int> arr = {1, 3, 5, 7, 9, 11, 13, 15, 17};
    int target = 9;
    int result = binarySearch(arr, target);
    if (result != -1) {
        cout << "Element found at index: " << result << endl;
    } else {
        cout << "Element not found." << endl;
    }
    return 0;
}
```

Variations of Binary Search:

1. **Recursive Binary Search**: Instead of using a loop, Binary Search can be implemented recursively.

   o The recursive approach works by calling the function on the left or right subarray depending on the comparison.

Example (Recursive Binary Search):

cpp

```cpp
int binarySearchRecursive(const vector<int>& arr, int left, int right, int target) {
    if (left > right) {
        return -1; // Base case: target not found
    }

    int mid = left + (right - left) / 2;

    if (arr[mid] == target) {
        return mid; // Target found
    } else if (arr[mid] > target) {
        return binarySearchRecursive(arr, left, mid - 1, target); // Search in left half
    } else {
        return binarySearchRecursive(arr, mid + 1, right, target); // Search in right half
    }
}
```

2. **Ternary Search**: This is a variation of Binary Search where the search interval is divided into three parts instead of two. It is less efficient than Binary Search in practice but can sometimes be used when dividing into three intervals makes sense for the problem at hand.

3. **Exponential Search**: Exponential Search is used when the size of the search space is not known in advance. It first finds the range by repeatedly doubling the size of the search space and then applies Binary Search on that range.

Searching in Sorted vs Unsorted Data

The efficiency of a search algorithm heavily depends on whether the data is sorted or unsorted:

1. **Searching in Sorted Data**:
    - **Binary Search** is highly efficient for searching sorted data, as its time complexity is logarithmic ($O(\log n)$).
    - Sorted data allows for efficient algorithms like **Binary Search** to reduce the search space exponentially.

2. **Searching in Unsorted Data**:
    - For **unsorted data**, you cannot use Binary Search because the data is not ordered.

- o The most common approach for unsorted data is **Linear Search**, which checks each element sequentially from the beginning of the list to the end.

Time Complexity of Linear Search:

- o **Worst-case**: O(n), because each element must be checked.
- o **Best-case**: O(1), if the first element is the target.
- o **Average-case**: O(n).

Example (Linear Search for Unsorted Data):

cpp

```cpp
#include <iostream>
#include <vector>
using namespace std;

int linearSearch(const vector<int>& arr, int target) {
    for (int i = 0; i < arr.size(); i++) {
        if (arr[i] == target) {
            return i; // Target found
        }
    }
    return -1; // Target not found
}

int main() {
```

```
vector<int> arr = {5, 2, 9, 3, 6, 8};
int target = 9;
int result = linearSearch(arr, target);
if (result != -1) {
    cout << "Element found at index: " << result << endl;
} else {
    cout << "Element not found." << endl;
}
return 0;
}
```

For unsorted data, you could also consider **Hash Tables** or **Binary Search Trees (BSTs)**, which allow for faster lookups in specific circumstances. However, they require additional data structures and upfront complexity in their implementation.

Real-World Example: Implementing Binary Search for a Database Query

Imagine you're working on a **database query system** where you need to find a specific record from a sorted list of customer IDs. This could be a customer database, with millions of records sorted by customer ID. Instead of looping through each record (which would be slow), you can use **Binary Search** to quickly locate the record, drastically reducing query time.

In the context of a **database query**, the steps could look like this:

1. The list of customer IDs is sorted in ascending order.
2. The target ID is provided by the user.

3. Use Binary Search to find the target ID in the sorted list of customer IDs.

Steps:

- If the database is large, instead of loading all records at once, you can perform a **range query** using Binary Search to narrow down the range of records.
- Once the target customer ID is located, return the corresponding customer information (name, address, etc.).

This approach is much more efficient than linearly scanning through every record in the database.

Example (Database-like Binary Search):

cpp

```
#include <iostream>
#include <vector>
using namespace std;

struct Customer {
    int id;
    string name;
};

int binarySearchDatabase(const vector<Customer>& db, int targetID) {
    int left = 0, right = db.size() - 1;
```

```cpp
    while (left <= right) {
        int mid = left + (right - left) / 2;

        if (db[mid].id == targetID) {
            return mid; // Target found
        } else if (db[mid].id < targetID) {
            left = mid + 1;
        } else {
            right = mid - 1;
        }
    }
    return -1; // Target not found
}

int main() {
    vector<Customer> database = {
        {1, "Alice"}, {2, "Bob"}, {3, "Charlie"}, {4, "David"}, {5, "Eve"}
    };
    int targetID = 3;

    int result = binarySearchDatabase(database, targetID);
    if (result != -1) {
        cout << "Customer found: " << database[result].name << endl;
    } else {
        cout << "Customer not found." << endl;
    }
    return 0;
}
```

In this chapter, we explored **Binary Search**, one of the most efficient searching algorithms for sorted data, along with its variations, such as **Recursive Binary Search** and **Ternary Search**. We also compared **Binary Search** with **Linear Search** for unsorted data, demonstrating the significant performance difference between searching in sorted and unsorted datasets. Lastly, we saw how Binary Search can be used in real-world applications like **database queries** to efficiently find records in large datasets.

In the next chapter, we'll explore more advanced search algorithms, such as **Hash Tables** and **Search Trees**, and how they are used to optimize data retrieval in more complex scenarios.

Chapter 5: Data Structures for Algorithm Optimization

In this chapter, we'll explore the crucial role that **data structures** play in optimizing algorithms. Choosing the right data structure for your problem is one of the most significant factors in improving the efficiency of your algorithm. We'll dive into some **advanced data structures**, including **trees**, **graphs**, **heaps**, and **hash tables**, each of which has distinct use cases that can make a huge difference in your program's performance. Lastly, we'll examine a real-world example of using a **hash table** for fast lookups.

The Importance of Choosing the Right Data Structure

A **data structure** is a way of organizing and storing data so that it can be accessed and modified efficiently. The choice of data structure affects the performance of algorithms in terms of time and space complexity. Using the wrong data structure for a problem can lead to inefficient algorithms, even if the algorithm itself is optimal.

For example:

- **Arrays** are simple and fast for index-based access but inefficient when it comes to inserting or deleting elements in the middle.

- **Linked lists** allow for faster insertions and deletions, but they are slower when accessing elements by index.
- **Hash tables** provide constant time complexity for lookups but may waste space and require handling hash collisions.
- **Trees** can optimize search, insertion, and deletion operations but may involve more complex memory management.

The key takeaway is that the selection of the right data structure is highly context-dependent and directly affects both time and space complexities.

Advanced Data Structures

In this section, we will dive into some advanced data structures that are widely used to optimize algorithms for specific types of problems.

1. **Trees**: A **tree** is a hierarchical data structure where each element is called a node. Each node contains a value and has pointers to its child nodes. The topmost node is called the **root**.

   Binary Trees are the simplest form of trees, where each node has at most two children: a left and a right child.

   o **Binary Search Trees (BST)**: A binary tree in which the left subtree of a node contains only nodes with keys less than the node's key, and the right subtree contains only nodes with keys greater than the node's key. This allows for efficient searching, insertion, and deletion in O(log n) time.

- o **Balanced Trees (AVL Tree, Red-Black Tree)**: These trees maintain balance, ensuring that the height remains logarithmic, thus preventing performance degradation.

Real-world Example: A **binary search tree** can be used in applications that require fast lookup, insertion, and deletion operations, like implementing a dictionary.

Time Complexity:

- o Searching: O(log n) (in balanced trees)
- o Insertion/Deletion: O(log n)

2. **Graphs**: A **graph** is a collection of nodes (also called vertices) connected by edges. Graphs are useful for modeling networks, such as social networks, road maps, and recommendation systems.

- o **Directed vs Undirected Graphs**: In a **directed graph**, the edges have a direction (e.g., a one-way street), while in an **undirected graph**, the edges don't have direction (e.g., a two-way street).

o **Weighted vs Unweighted Graphs**: A **weighted graph** assigns a weight to each edge, while in an **unweighted graph**, all edges are considered equal.

Applications: Graphs are used in algorithms like **Dijkstra's shortest path**, **Depth-First Search (DFS)**, and **Breadth-First Search (BFS)**.

Time Complexity:

o BFS/DFS (adjacency list representation): O(V + E), where V is the number of vertices and E is the number of edges.

o Dijkstra's Algorithm (with priority queue): O(E log V)

3. **Heaps**: A **heap** is a specialized tree-based data structure that satisfies the **heap property**. The heap property ensures that the value of the parent node is either greater than or smaller than the value of its child nodes, depending on whether it is a **max-heap** or **min-heap**.

o **Max-Heap**: The parent node's value is greater than or equal to the values of its children. This is useful for **priority queues**.

o **Min-Heap**: The parent node's value is less than or equal to the values of its children. This is also useful for **priority queues** and finding the smallest element in a collection.

Applications: Heaps are widely used for efficient **priority queue** implementations, and algorithms like **Heap Sort** and **Dijkstra's shortest path**.

Time Complexity:

- o Insert: O(log n)
- o Extract-Min/Max: O(log n)

4. **Hash Tables**: A **hash table** is a data structure that stores key-value pairs. It uses a **hash function** to compute an index (hash value) into an array of buckets or slots, from which the desired value can be found.

Applications: Hash tables are used to implement **hash maps**, **sets**, and **caches**, enabling fast lookups, insertions, and deletions.

- o **Handling Collisions**: If two keys hash to the same index (a collision), hash tables use methods like **chaining** (storing multiple elements at the same index using linked lists) or **open addressing** (finding another available spot within the array).

Time Complexity:

- o Average-case: O(1) for lookups, insertions, and deletions.
- o Worst-case (due to collisions): O(n), but this can be mitigated with a good hash function.

Real-World Example: Using a Hash Table for Fast Lookups

Imagine you're building a **web application** where users can search for products from a catalog of thousands of items. You need a way to quickly find a product based on its unique identifier (e.g., product ID). A **hash table** is a perfect solution for this problem due to its average O(1) time complexity for lookups.

Here's a real-world example of how you can use a **hash table** for fast lookups in a product catalog:

1. **Use Case**: You have a large catalog of products, each identified by a unique product ID. A customer enters the product ID to search for a specific product.
2. **Solution**: Implement a **hash table** to store product IDs as keys and product details (name, description, price, etc.) as values. When a customer searches for a product by ID, you can retrieve the product details in constant time.

Code Example (using unordered_map in C++):

cpp

```
#include <iostream>
```

```cpp
#include <unordered_map>
#include <string>
using namespace std;

struct Product {
    string name;
    double price;
};

int main() {
    // Create a hash table (unordered_map) for storing products
    unordered_map<int, Product> productCatalog;

    // Adding products to the hash table
    productCatalog[101] = {"Smartphone", 499.99};
    productCatalog[102] = {"Laptop", 899.99};
    productCatalog[103] = {"Headphones", 79.99};

    // Searching for a product by its ID
    int productID = 102;
    if (productCatalog.find(productID) != productCatalog.end()) {
        cout << "Product found: " << productCatalog[productID].name << endl;
        cout << "Price: $" << productCatalog[productID].price << endl;
    } else {
        cout << "Product not found!" << endl;
    }

    return 0;
}
```

Explanation:

- The unordered_map is a hash table where the product ID is the key, and the Product struct holds the product details.
- When a user searches for a product by its ID, the lookup operation is performed in $O(1)$ time, making it extremely fast.

In large-scale applications like e-commerce platforms, using a hash table for fast lookups ensures the system remains responsive and scalable, even with millions of products in the catalog.

In this chapter, we covered the importance of choosing the right data structure to optimize algorithms. We examined several **advanced data structures**:

- **Trees**, including **binary search trees** and **balanced trees**, for fast searches, insertions, and deletions.
- **Graphs**, for modeling complex relationships and networks.
- **Heaps**, for implementing efficient **priority queues**.
- **Hash tables**, for fast lookups and efficient handling of key-value pairs.

We also provided a real-world example of using a **hash table** to enable fast lookups in an e-commerce platform. In the next chapter, we will explore **Dynamic Programming** and how it can be used to optimize solutions for complex problems.

Chapter 6: Dynamic Programming: The Basics

Dynamic Programming (DP) is a powerful algorithmic technique used to solve complex problems by breaking them down into simpler subproblems. It is particularly useful when the problem can be divided into overlapping subproblems, where the same subproblems are solved multiple times. DP avoids the redundant computation of subproblems by storing their solutions, making it more efficient than other approaches like recursion.

In this chapter, we'll introduce the basics of dynamic programming, explain how it improves time complexity, and show how to solve a well-known problem, the **Fibonacci sequence**, using DP.

Introduction to Dynamic Programming (DP)

Dynamic programming is a method for solving problems by solving each subproblem just once and storing its solution. This approach eliminates the need for recomputing solutions for overlapping subproblems. The two main approaches to DP are:

1. **Top-down approach (Memoization)**: This method starts solving the problem by breaking it into subproblems recursively. When a subproblem is solved, its result is stored (usually in an array or hash table) so that it can be reused whenever needed, rather than recalculating it.

2. **Bottom-up approach (Tabulation)**: This method solves all possible subproblems first, starting from the simplest ones and building up to the solution of the main problem. It iteratively solves subproblems and uses their solutions to solve larger problems.

The core idea of dynamic programming is to **optimize** a problem by avoiding repeated calculations. This is particularly effective in problems with overlapping subproblems and optimal substructure, where the solution to a problem can be constructed from solutions to smaller subproblems.

How DP Improves Time Complexity by Storing Intermediate Results

One of the most significant advantages of dynamic programming is its ability to store intermediate results, thus reducing the time complexity of problems that would otherwise involve repeated calculations.

Let's consider a simple recursive solution for the **Fibonacci sequence**:

- The **Fibonacci sequence** is defined as: $F(n)=F(n-1)+F(n-2)F(n) = F(n-1) + F(n-2)F(n)=F(n-1)+F(n-2)$ with base cases: $F(0)=0, F(1)=1F(0) = 0, \quad F(1) = 1F(0)=0, F(1)=1$ A naive recursive solution calculates $F(n)$ by calling $F(n-1)$ and $F(n-2)$

recursively, resulting in redundant computations. For example, F(3) requires calculating F(2), which in turn requires recalculating F(1) and F(0) multiple times.

Time Complexity of Naive Recursion: In the naive recursive solution, the time complexity is exponential, specifically $O(2n)O(2^\wedge n)O(2n)$, because each function call results in two more function calls.

Dynamic programming improves this by **storing the results** of subproblems in an array or table, so that the next time a subproblem needs to be solved, it can simply look up the answer in constant time. This reduces the time complexity significantly.

Time Complexity of DP (Memoization/Tabulation): By storing intermediate results, the time complexity is reduced to $O(n)O(n)O(n)$, as each subproblem is solved only once.

Real-World Example: Solving the Fibonacci Sequence Using DP
Let's demonstrate how dynamic programming improves the solution to the Fibonacci sequence problem. We will first look at the **naive recursive approach** and then compare it with the **DP approach**.

Naive Recursive Approach (Without DP)
The recursive approach directly implements the Fibonacci formula:

cpp

```cpp
#include <iostream>
using namespace std;

int fibonacci(int n) {
    if (n <= 1) {
        return n;
    }
    return fibonacci(n-1) + fibonacci(n-2);
}

int main() {
    int n = 10;  // Calculate the 10th Fibonacci number
    cout << "Fibonacci(" << n << ") = " << fibonacci(n) << endl;
    return 0;
}
```

Explanation:

- The function fibonacci(n) recursively calls itself to compute F(n-1) and F(n-2).
- This approach recalculates the same Fibonacci values many times, resulting in inefficient performance.

Time Complexity:

- The time complexity of this naive recursive approach is $O(2n)O(2^n)O(2n)$, because of the redundant recalculations.

DP Approach (Memoization)

Now, let's implement the Fibonacci sequence using dynamic programming with **memoization**. We will store the results of subproblems in an array and reuse them.

cpp

```cpp
#include <iostream>
#include <vector>
using namespace std;

int fibonacci(int n, vector<int>& memo) {
    if (n <= 1) {
        return n;
    }
    if (memo[n] != -1) {
        return memo[n];  // Return already computed result
    }
    memo[n] = fibonacci(n-1, memo) + fibonacci(n-2, memo);  // Store the result
    return memo[n];
}

int main() {
    int n = 10;  // Calculate the 10th Fibonacci number
    vector<int> memo(n+1, -1);  // Initialize memoization array with -1
    cout << "Fibonacci(" << n << ") = " << fibonacci(n, memo) << endl;
    return 0;
}
```

Explanation:

- We use a vector memo to store the Fibonacci values as we compute them.
- The function checks if the value of fibonacci(n) has already been calculated (i.e., memo[n] is not -1). If it has, it simply returns the stored value.
- If the value hasn't been calculated, it computes it recursively, stores the result, and returns it.

Time Complexity:

- The time complexity of the memoization approach is $O(n)O(n)O(n)$, since each Fibonacci number is computed only once and then stored for reuse.

DP Approach (Tabulation)

We can also solve the Fibonacci problem using **bottom-up tabulation**. In this approach, we iteratively compute all Fibonacci numbers up to n, starting from the base cases.

cpp

```
#include <iostream>
using namespace std;

int fibonacci(int n) {
  if (n <= 1) {
    return n;
  }
}
```

```cpp
    int dp[n+1];
    dp[0] = 0;  // Base case
    dp[1] = 1;  // Base case

    for (int i = 2; i <= n; i++) {
        dp[i] = dp[i-1] + dp[i-2];  // Build up from the bottom
    }

    return dp[n];
}

int main() {
    int n = 10;  // Calculate the 10th Fibonacci number
    cout << "Fibonacci(" << n << ") = " << fibonacci(n) << endl;
    return 0;
}
```

Explanation:

- We initialize a dp array where dp[i] stores the Fibonacci number for i.
- We compute the Fibonacci numbers iteratively, starting from the base cases (dp[0] = 0 and dp[1] = 1), and fill the array up to dp[n].

Time Complexity:

- The time complexity of the tabulation approach is $O(n)O(n)O(n)$, and the space complexity is also

$O(n)O(n)O(n)$, since we are storing all Fibonacci numbers from 0 to n.

Why Use DP for Fibonacci?

While the naive recursive approach is easy to understand, it's inefficient for large n because of repeated calculations. **Dynamic programming** solves this problem by storing intermediate results, allowing the solution to be computed in linear time.

- **Memoization** improves the recursive solution by storing results for each subproblem.
- **Tabulation** avoids recursion and iteratively builds up the solution, often being more efficient in terms of space usage.

In both cases, the time complexity is reduced from $O(2n)O(2\wedge n)O(2n)$ to $O(n)O(n)O(n)$, which is a significant improvement.

Dynamic programming is a crucial technique for optimizing algorithms by solving problems that can be broken down into overlapping subproblems. By storing intermediate results, DP significantly reduces time complexity compared to naive recursive solutions. We demonstrated this with the **Fibonacci sequence** problem, showing how both memoization and tabulation can be used to solve it efficiently in $O(n)O(n)O(n)$ time.

In the next chapter, we will explore **Greedy Algorithms** and how they provide efficient solutions to optimization problems.

Chapter 7: Advanced Dynamic Programming

Dynamic programming (DP) is one of the most powerful techniques in algorithm design, particularly for solving problems that involve optimal decisions over time or complex subproblems. In this chapter, we will build on the fundamentals of DP and explore advanced techniques, optimization strategies, and how to apply DP to more complex problems, such as the **Knapsack problem** and the **Longest Common Subsequence** (LCS).

We will also look at real-world examples where dynamic programming can be used to solve optimization problems, particularly in resource allocation.

Advanced DP Techniques

As we've seen, dynamic programming relies on two main approaches: **Memoization** (top-down approach) and **Tabulation** (bottom-up approach). However, there are several optimization techniques and strategies that can further enhance the efficiency of dynamic programming algorithms.

1. **Memoization vs. Tabulation:**
   - **Memoization** stores results of subproblems as they are computed, and it works recursively. While it's

easy to implement, the recursion overhead can be costly in terms of function calls and stack space.

- o **Tabulation**, on the other hand, uses an iterative approach to build up the solution from the base cases. It avoids recursion overhead but requires initializing and managing an entire table for the subproblem solutions.

2. **Space Optimization in DP:**

- o Many DP problems require a full table to store results of subproblems. However, if a problem only requires results from a few previous states (rather than all states), you can optimize space usage. Instead of maintaining a full 2D table, for example, you might only need to store the current and previous rows (or columns), reducing space complexity.

- o **Example:** The **Fibonacci sequence** solution can be optimized to use just two variables for storing the current and previous values instead of an entire array or table.

3. **Bitmasking:**

- o Bitmasking is a technique used in DP to represent a set of items using bits. This technique can optimize problems that involve subsets, like the **Travelling Salesman Problem (TSP)** or problems involving combinations of sets. By using a bitmask to represent subsets, we reduce the need for multiple arrays, simplifying the state representation and reducing memory consumption.

4. **DP with Rolling Arrays:**

   o   When solving a problem where the solution at any state only depends on a few previous states (e.g., only the last row or column of a DP table), we can use a rolling array. By keeping only the last few states in memory, we can reduce the space complexity while still preserving the functionality of the DP algorithm.

Solving Complex DP Problems

Now, let's explore two well-known and complex problems in dynamic programming: the **Knapsack problem** and the **Longest Common Subsequence** (LCS). We will discuss the principles behind these problems, how DP can be applied to solve them, and provide real-world examples.

---

1. Knapsack Problem

The **Knapsack problem** is one of the most famous optimization problems, and it comes in many variations, such as the 0/1 Knapsack problem. The general problem involves selecting a subset of items with given weights and values to maximize the total value without exceeding the capacity of the knapsack.

Problem Statement:

You are given a set of items, each with a weight and a value. You also have a knapsack that can carry a certain weight. The goal is to determine the maximum value you can carry in the knapsack without exceeding its weight capacity.

Dynamic Programming Approach:

We can solve the 0/1 Knapsack problem using dynamic programming by constructing a table where each entry represents the maximum value we can achieve with a certain weight capacity.

- Let's define a DP table dp[i][w], where:
  - i represents the number of items considered.
  - w represents the current weight capacity of the knapsack.
  - dp[i][w] stores the maximum value obtainable by considering the first i items with a weight capacity of w.

The recursive relation is:

- If the weight of the current item is greater than the current capacity w, we cannot include the item, so: dp[i][w]=dp[i−1][w]dp[i][w] = dp[i−1][w]dp[i][w]=dp[i−1][w]

- Otherwise, we have two choices: either we include the item, or we don't. The recurrence relation becomes: dp[i][w]=max⁡(dp[i−1][w],dp[i−1][w−weight[i−1]]+value[i−1])dp[i][w] = \max(dp[i-1][w], dp[i-1][w-\text{weight}[i-1]] + \text{value}[i-1])dp[i][w]=max(dp[i−1][w],dp[i−1][w−weight[i−1]]+value[i−1])

Code Example:

cpp

```cpp
#include <iostream>
#include <vector>
using namespace std;

int knapsack(int W, vector<int>& weights, vector<int>& values, int n) {
    vector<vector<int>> dp(n+1, vector<int>(W+1, 0));

    for (int i = 1; i <= n; i++) {
        for (int w = 1; w <= W; w++) {
            if (weights[i-1] <= w) {
                dp[i][w] = max(dp[i-1][w], dp[i-1][w-weights[i-1]] + values[i-1]);
            } else {
                dp[i][w] = dp[i-1][w];
```

```
        }
      }
    }
    return dp[n][W];
}

int main() {
    int W = 50;  // Knapsack capacity
    vector<int> weights = {10, 20, 30};  // Weights of items
    vector<int> values = {60, 100, 120};  // Values of items
    int n = weights.size();  // Number of items

    cout << "Maximum value in Knapsack: " << knapsack(W, weights, values, n) << endl;
    return 0;
}
```

Explanation:

- We create a DP table dp of size (n+1) x (W+1), where n is the number of items and W is the knapsack capacity.
- For each item, we check if it can fit in the knapsack (i.e., its weight is less than or equal to the current capacity w). We update the DP table by considering whether including the item results in a higher value.

Time Complexity: $O(n \times W)$, where n is the number of items, and W is the knapsack capacity.

2. Longest Common Subsequence (LCS)

The **Longest Common Subsequence** problem asks for the longest subsequence that appears in the same order in both strings. Unlike substrings, subsequences do not need to be contiguous.

Problem Statement:
Given two strings X and Y, find the length of the longest subsequence that appears in both X and Y.

Dynamic Programming Approach:
We solve the LCS problem by constructing a table dp where dp[i][j] represents the length of the LCS of the first i characters of string X and the first j characters of string Y.

The recurrence relation is:

- If the characters X[i-1] and Y[j-1] match, we extend the LCS by 1: dp[i][j]=dp[i−1][j−1]+1dp[i][j] = dp[i-1][j-1] + 1dp[i][j]=dp[i−1][j−1]+1

- Otherwise, we take the maximum LCS length from either excluding the current character of X or excluding the current character of Y: dp[i][j]=max⁡(dp[i−1][j],dp[i][j−1])dp[i][j] = \max(dp[i-1][j], dp[i][j-1])dp[i][j]=max(dp[i−1][j],dp[i][j−1])

Code Example:
cpp

```cpp
#include <iostream>
#include <vector>
#include <string>
using namespace std;

int lcs(string X, string Y) {
    int m = X.length(), n = Y.length();
    vector<vector<int>> dp(m+1, vector<int>(n+1, 0));

    for (int i = 1; i <= m; i++) {
        for (int j = 1; j <= n; j++) {
            if (X[i-1] == Y[j-1]) {
                dp[i][j] = dp[i-1][j-1] + 1;
            } else {
                dp[i][j] = max(dp[i-1][j], dp[i][j-1]);
            }
        }
    }
    return dp[m][n];
}

int main() {
    string X = "AGGTAB";
    string Y = "GXTXAYB";

    cout << "Length of Longest Common Subsequence: " << lcs(X, Y) << endl;
    return 0;
}
```

Explanation:

- We build a DP table dp, where each entry dp[i][j] represents the length of the LCS for the first i characters of X and the first j characters of Y.
- If the characters match, we add 1 to the previous LCS length; otherwise, we take the maximum length from either the previous row or column.

Time Complexity: $O(m \times n)$$O(m \times n)$$O(m \times n)$, where m and n are the lengths of the two input strings.

Real-World Example: Solving an Optimal Resource Allocation Problem

Let's apply dynamic programming to an **optimal resource allocation problem** where we need to allocate resources across multiple projects to maximize profit, subject to a budget constraint.

The problem can be framed similarly to the **Knapsack problem**. Each project has a cost (weight) and a profit (value), and we want to maximize the total profit without exceeding a given budget.

- **Budget** = Total resources available.
- **Projects** = Items in the knapsack, with each project having a cost and a profit.

- The objective is to maximize the total profit by selecting a combination of projects that do not exceed the budget.

We can solve this problem using the **Knapsack DP approach** we discussed earlier.

In this chapter, we covered advanced dynamic programming techniques such as memoization, tabulation, and space optimization. We also delved into solving complex DP problems like the **Knapsack problem** and the **Longest Common Subsequence**, providing a deeper understanding of how DP can be applied to real-world scenarios, such as optimal resource allocation.

Understanding these advanced techniques allows you to tackle a wider range of optimization problems with dynamic programming, making it an essential tool in your problem-solving toolkit.

Chapter 8: Greedy Algorithms

Greedy algorithms are a class of algorithms that follow the *greedy approach*, meaning they make a sequence of choices, each of which looks best at the moment. The key idea is to choose the optimal solution at each step, with the hope that these local optimum choices will lead to a global optimum solution. While greedy algorithms are often very efficient and easy to implement, they don't always produce the best solution for all problems. In this chapter, we will explore greedy algorithms, understand when they are appropriate, and examine a few classic problems where they shine.

Understanding Greedy Algorithms and When They Are Appropriate

A **greedy algorithm** works by making the locally optimal choice at each step, with the hope that these choices will lead to the global optimum. This approach is usually much faster than other algorithms, like dynamic programming or brute force, because it doesn't have to explore all possible solutions.

However, a greedy algorithm does not always guarantee the best solution for all problems. The key to using greedy algorithms effectively is determining if the problem exhibits the **greedy-choice property** and the **optimal substructure**:

1. **Greedy-Choice Property**: A problem has the greedy-choice property if a locally optimal choice at each step leads to a globally optimal solution.

2. **Optimal Substructure**: The problem can be broken down into smaller subproblems, each of which has an optimal solution.

Greedy algorithms are best suited for problems where these two properties hold. In contrast, for problems that don't exhibit these properties, a greedy approach might fail to find the best solution, and other methods (like dynamic programming) should be considered.

Common Greedy Algorithms and Examples

Let's take a look at two classic problems where greedy algorithms are effective: the **Fractional Knapsack problem** and the **Activity Selection problem**.

---

1. Fractional Knapsack Problem

In the **Fractional Knapsack problem**, we are given a set of items, each with a weight and a value, and a knapsack that can carry a certain weight. The goal is to maximize the total value in the knapsack, but we can take fractions of items (as opposed to the 0/1

Knapsack problem, where we must take an entire item or none at all).

Problem Statement:

- You are given a set of n items, each with a weight w_i and a value v_i.
- You have a knapsack with capacity W.
- You are allowed to take fractions of items.
- Find the maximum value you can carry in the knapsack.

Greedy Strategy:

- The key idea in solving the Fractional Knapsack problem is to take items based on their **value-to-weight ratio** (v_i / w_i), and prioritize taking the items with the highest ratio first.
- The algorithm works by sorting the items based on their value-to-weight ratio in descending order. Then, we take the item with the highest ratio, fill the knapsack as much as possible, and continue with the next item until the knapsack is full.

Code Example:

cpp

```
#include <iostream>
#include <vector>
#include <algorithm>
```

```
using namespace std;

struct Item {
    int weight;
    int value;
    double ratio;
};

bool compare(Item a, Item b) {
    return a.ratio > b.ratio;  // Sort items by value-to-weight ratio in descending
order
}

double fractionalKnapsack(int W, vector<Item>& items) {
    sort(items.begin(), items.end(), compare);
    double totalValue = 0.0;

    for (auto& item : items) {
        if (W == 0) break;

        // Take as much as possible of the item
        if (item.weight <= W) {
            W -= item.weight;
            totalValue += item.value;
        } else {
            totalValue += item.value * ((double)W / item.weight);
            break;  // Knapsack is full
        }
    }
```

```
    return totalValue;
}

int main() {
    int W = 50;  // Knapsack capacity
    vector<Item> items = {{10, 60, 0}, {20, 100, 0}, {30, 120, 0}};

    for (auto& item : items) {
        item.ratio = (double)item.value / item.weight;  // Calculate value-to-weight
ratio
    }

    cout << "Maximum value in Knapsack: " << fractionalKnapsack(W, items)
<< endl;
    return 0;
}
```

Explanation:

- We first calculate the value-to-weight ratio for each item.
- Then, we sort the items by this ratio and begin filling the knapsack.
- If an item can fit completely, we take it whole; otherwise, we take the fraction that fits and stop once the knapsack is full.

Time Complexity: Sorting the items takes $O(n\log n)$, and filling the knapsack is $O(n)$, making the overall time complexity $O(n\log n)$.

2. Activity Selection Problem

The **Activity Selection Problem** involves selecting the maximum number of activities that don't overlap. Each activity has a start time and a finish time. The goal is to choose the largest number of activities that can be performed by a single person, given that they take a fixed amount of time and cannot be done simultaneously.

Problem Statement:

- You are given n activities, each with a start time and a finish time.
- The goal is to select the maximum number of non-overlapping activities.

Greedy Strategy:

- The greedy approach here is to select the activity that finishes the earliest, then choose the next activity that starts after the current one finishes, and so on.
- By selecting the earliest finishing activity, we leave as much room as possible for other activities.

Code Example:

cpp

```cpp
#include <iostream>
#include <vector>
#include <algorithm>
using namespace std;

struct Activity {
    int start;
    int finish;
};

bool compare(Activity a, Activity b) {
    return a.finish < b.finish;  // Sort activities by finish time in ascending order
}

vector<Activity> activitySelection(vector<Activity>& activities) {
    sort(activities.begin(), activities.end(), compare);

    vector<Activity> selectedActivities;
    selectedActivities.push_back(activities[0]);  // Select the first activity

    int lastFinishTime = activities[0].finish;

    for (int i = 1; i < activities.size(); i++) {
        if (activities[i].start >= lastFinishTime) {
            selectedActivities.push_back(activities[i]);
            lastFinishTime = activities[i].finish;
        }
    }

    return selectedActivities;
```

```
}

int main() {
    vector<Activity> activities = {{1, 4}, {3, 5}, {0, 6}, {5, 7}, {8, 9}, {5, 9}};

    vector<Activity> selected = activitySelection(activities);

    cout << "Selected Activities:" << endl;
    for (auto& activity : selected) {
        cout << "(" << activity.start << ", " << activity.finish << ")" << endl;
    }
    return 0;
}
```

Explanation:

- The activities are first sorted by their finish times.
- Starting from the earliest finish time, we select activities whose start times are greater than or equal to the finish time of the last selected activity.
- This ensures that we select the maximum number of non-overlapping activities.

Time Complexity: Sorting the activities takes $O(n\log n)$ $O(n \log n)$ $O(nlogn)$, and selecting the activities takes $O(n)$ $O(n)$ $O(n)$, making the overall time complexity $O(n\log n)$ $O(n \log n)$ $O(nlogn)$.

Real-World Example: Optimizing Job Scheduling

One of the most practical applications of greedy algorithms is in **job scheduling**, where we need to schedule jobs to maximize efficiency or minimize resource usage. A classic example is scheduling jobs on a single machine where each job has a start time, finish time, and a profit associated with it.

In this case, the greedy algorithm would involve:

1. Sorting jobs based on their finish times.
2. Scheduling jobs such that we can accommodate as many jobs as possible, without overlap, to maximize the total profit.

By applying a greedy algorithm, we ensure that jobs are scheduled in the most efficient way possible, minimizing idle time and maximizing throughput.

In this chapter, we've explored **greedy algorithms**, which make locally optimal choices at each step in the hope of finding a globally optimal solution. We've covered two classic problems: the **Fractional Knapsack problem** and the **Activity Selection problem**, demonstrating how greedy algorithms work in practice. Additionally, we've applied these concepts to a **job scheduling**

problem, showing how greedy approaches can be used to solve real-world optimization problems efficiently.

While greedy algorithms are often faster and simpler to implement than dynamic programming, they are not always the best choice. It is crucial to determine whether the problem exhibits the greedy-choice property and optimal substructure before opting for a greedy approach. In cases where these properties hold, greedy algorithms can provide an elegant and efficient solution.

Chapter 9: Backtracking Algorithms

Backtracking is a powerful algorithmic technique used for solving problems where finding the optimal solution requires exploring all possibilities, but with the ability to abandon paths that don't lead to a solution early in the process. It is especially useful for problems that involve **combinatorial search** and **constraint satisfaction**, where the solution space is large and needs to be navigated efficiently by pruning invalid paths.

What is Backtracking, and How Does It Work?

Backtracking can be described as a **depth-first search** approach, where we try to build a solution incrementally. At each step, we make a decision, and if we find that this decision doesn't lead to a valid solution, we backtrack—undoing the previous decision and trying an alternative.

In other words, backtracking systematically explores all possible solutions to a problem, and when it detects that a solution path is not viable, it backs up to the previous step and tries another option. This process continues until a valid solution is found or all options are exhausted.

The key steps involved in a backtracking algorithm are:

1. **Make a choice**: Choose a possibility to continue the solution.

2. **Explore**: Proceed to the next step based on the choice.

3. **Check validity**: If the solution doesn't violate the problem's constraints, continue.

4. **Backtrack**: If a step leads to an invalid solution, undo the last choice and try another.

Backtracking algorithms are often used in problems where you need to check all possible configurations but can discard certain paths based on some constraints.

Solving Problems Using Backtracking

Let's dive into two well-known problems that are typically solved using backtracking:

1. **N-Queens Problem**: Placing N queens on an NxN chessboard such that no two queens threaten each other.

2. **Sudoku Solver**: Filling a partially completed Sudoku grid such that the final configuration satisfies the constraints of the game.

---

1. N-Queens Problem

The **N-Queens problem** involves placing N queens on an N x N chessboard such that no two queens threaten each other. A queen can attack another queen if they share the same row, column, or diagonal.

Problem Statement:

- Given an integer N, place N queens on an N x N chessboard so that no two queens are in the same row, column, or diagonal.

Backtracking Approach:

1. We place a queen in a row and check if the current placement is valid (i.e., no other queen is in the same column or diagonal).
2. If the placement is valid, we recursively attempt to place the queen in the next row.
3. If placing the queen leads to a conflict later on, we backtrack by removing the queen and trying the next column.
4. We repeat the process until all queens are placed validly or all possibilities are exhausted.

Code Example:

cpp

```cpp
#include <iostream>
#include <vector>
using namespace std;

bool isSafe(int row, int col, vector<vector<int>>& board, int N) {
    for (int i = 0; i < row; i++) {
        if (board[i][col] == 1) return false; // Check column
        if (col - (row - i) >= 0 && board[i][col - (row - i)] == 1) return false; //
Check upper left diagonal
        if (col + (row - i) < N && board[i][col + (row - i)] == 1) return false; //
Check upper right diagonal
    }
    return true;
}

bool solveNQueens(int row, vector<vector<int>>& board, int N) {
    if (row == N) return true; // All queens are placed

    for (int col = 0; col < N; col++) {
        if (isSafe(row, col, board, N)) {
            board[row][col] = 1; // Place queen
            if (solveNQueens(row + 1, board, N)) return true; // Recurse to place
next queen
            board[row][col] = 0; // Backtrack
        }
    }
    return false; // No valid position found
}

void printBoard(vector<vector<int>>& board, int N) {
```

```cpp
    for (int i = 0; i < N; i++) {
        for (int j = 0; j < N; j++) {
            cout << (board[i][j] ? "Q " : ". ");
        }
        cout << endl;
    }
}

int main() {
    int N = 8;  // For 8 queens
    vector<vector<int>> board(N, vector<int>(N, 0));

    if (solveNQueens(0, board, N)) {
        printBoard(board, N);
    } else {
        cout << "Solution does not exist" << endl;
    }
    return 0;
}
```

Explanation:

- The algorithm starts by placing a queen in the first row and checks for valid placement.
- If valid, it places the queen in the next row and repeats the process.
- If it reaches a row where no valid positions are possible, it backtracks and tries a new position for the queen in the previous row.

- The process continues until all queens are placed or all possibilities are explored.

Time Complexity: The time complexity for the N-Queens problem using backtracking is $O(N!)O(N!)O(N!)$ because in the worst case, the algorithm tries every combination of placements.

---

2. Sudoku Solver

A **Sudoku** puzzle consists of a 9x9 grid, where some of the cells are filled with digits from 1 to 9, and the rest are empty. The goal is to fill the empty cells with numbers such that each row, each column, and each of the nine 3x3 subgrids contains all the digits from 1 to 9.

Problem Statement:

- You are given a partially filled Sudoku grid.
- Solve the puzzle by filling in the empty cells with numbers from 1 to 9.

Backtracking Approach:

1. Start with the first empty cell.
2. Try placing each number from 1 to 9 in the cell.

3. If the number is valid (doesn't violate the Sudoku rules), move to the next empty cell.

4. If we fill the entire grid successfully, we have a solution.

5. If placing a number leads to an invalid configuration later, backtrack by removing the number and trying the next possibility.

6. Repeat until the puzzle is solved or all possibilities are exhausted.

Code Example:

cpp

```cpp
#include <iostream>
#include <vector>
using namespace std;

bool isSafe(int row, int col, vector<vector<int>>& board, int num) {
    // Check the row
    for (int x = 0; x < 9; x++) {
        if (board[row][x] == num) return false;
    }

    // Check the column
    for (int x = 0; x < 9; x++) {
        if (board[x][col] == num) return false;
    }

    // Check the 3x3 grid
    int startRow = row - row % 3, startCol = col - col % 3;
```

```
    for (int i = 0; i < 3; i++) {
        for (int j = 0; j < 3; j++) {
            if (board[i + startRow][j + startCol] == num) return false;
        }
    }

    return true;
}


bool solveSudoku(vector<vector<int>>& board) {
    int row, col;
    bool emptyCellFound = false;

    for (row = 0; row < 9; row++) {
        for (col = 0; col < 9; col++) {
            if (board[row][col] == 0) {
                emptyCellFound = true;
                break;
            }
        }
        if (emptyCellFound) break;
    }

    if (!emptyCellFound) return true;  // Puzzle solved

    for (int num = 1; num <= 9; num++) {
        if (isSafe(row, col, board, num)) {
            board[row][col] = num;
            if (solveSudoku(board)) return true;
            board[row][col] = 0;  // Backtrack
```

```
      }
   }

   return false;  // No solution
}

void printBoard(vector<vector<int>>& board) {
   for (int i = 0; i < 9; i++) {
      for (int j = 0; j < 9; j++) {
         cout << board[i][j] << " ";
      }
      cout << endl;
   }
}

int main() {
   vector<vector<int>> board = {
      {5, 3, 0, 0, 7, 0, 0, 0, 0},
      {6, 0, 0, 1, 9, 5, 0, 0, 0},
      {0, 9, 8, 0, 0, 0, 0, 6, 0},
      {8, 0, 0, 0, 6, 0, 0, 0, 3},
      {4, 0, 0, 8, 0, 3, 0, 0, 1},
      {7, 0, 0, 0, 2, 0, 0,
```

Chapter 10: Graph Algorithms: Basics

Graphs are a fundamental data structure in computer science, used to represent relationships between objects. A graph consists of nodes (also called vertices) and edges (the connections between nodes). Graphs are versatile and are used to model real-world problems like social networks, transportation systems, dependency chains, and even the structure of the internet.

In this chapter, we will introduce the basic concepts of graphs, how to represent them in memory, and the foundational algorithms for traversing graphs: **Depth-First Search (DFS)** and **Breadth-First Search (BFS)**. These algorithms serve as the building blocks for more complex graph algorithms, and understanding them is essential for solving a variety of problems in computer science.

Introduction to Graphs: Representation and Types of Graphs
A **graph** consists of two main components:

1. **Nodes (Vertices)**: These represent the entities or objects in the graph.
2. **Edges**: These are the connections between the nodes and represent the relationships between the objects.

Graphs can be categorized into several types based on the properties of the edges:

- **Directed Graph (Digraph)**: In a directed graph, the edges have a direction, meaning they go from one node to another (e.g., a directed edge from node A to node B).
- **Undirected Graph**: In an undirected graph, the edges do not have a direction. If there is an edge between node A and node B, you can traverse from A to B and vice versa.
- **Weighted Graph**: In a weighted graph, each edge has a weight or cost associated with it. This is useful for modeling problems like finding the shortest path (e.g., road networks where each edge represents a road with a certain distance).
- **Unweighted Graph**: An unweighted graph does not associate weights with its edges, meaning all edges are considered equal.
- **Cyclic vs. Acyclic Graph**: A graph is cyclic if it contains at least one cycle (a path where the first and last nodes are the same), and acyclic if no such cycle exists. If the graph is directed and acyclic, it's called a **Directed Acyclic Graph (DAG)**.

Depth-First Search (DFS) and Breadth-First Search (BFS)

Both **DFS** and **BFS** are algorithms used to traverse a graph. The key difference lies in the order in which the nodes are visited.

1. Depth-First Search (DFS)

DFS explores as far as possible along each branch before backtracking. It uses a **stack** to keep track of the nodes to visit next. DFS is particularly useful for searching through large, deep graphs where you need to explore each branch completely before moving to another branch.

Steps for DFS:

1. Start from the source node.
2. Visit the node and mark it as visited.
3. Explore the unvisited neighbors of the node.
4. Recursively visit each neighbor.
5. If you reach a dead-end (a node with no unvisited neighbors), backtrack and continue from the previous node.

DFS Implementation (Recursive):

cpp

```
#include <iostream>
#include <vector>
using namespace std;

class Graph {
    int V;  // Number of vertices
```

```cpp
    vector<vector<int>> adjList;  // Adjacency list representation of graph

public:
    Graph(int V);
    void addEdge(int u, int v);
    void DFS(int start);
    void DFSUtil(int v, vector<bool>& visited);
};

Graph::Graph(int V) {
    this->V = V;
    adjList.resize(V);
}

void Graph::addEdge(int u, int v) {
    adjList[u].push_back(v);
}

void Graph::DFSUtil(int v, vector<bool>& visited) {
    visited[v] = true;
    cout << v << " ";
    for (int neighbor : adjList[v]) {
        if (!visited[neighbor]) {
            DFSUtil(neighbor, visited);
        }
    }
}

void Graph::DFS(int start) {
    vector<bool> visited(V, false);
```

```
    DFSUtil(start, visited);
}

int main() {
    Graph g(6);
    g.addEdge(0, 1);
    g.addEdge(0, 2);
    g.addEdge(1, 3);
    g.addEdge(1, 4);
    g.addEdge(2, 5);

    cout << "DFS starting from node 0: ";
    g.DFS(0);

    return 0;
}
```

Explanation:

- In this example, the DFS function initializes a visited array and calls the helper function DFSUtil, which performs the depth-first traversal.
- The graph is represented using an **adjacency list** (a vector of vectors), and edges are added using the addEdge() function.
- Starting from node 0, the DFS explores the graph recursively.

Time Complexity: The time complexity of DFS is $O(V+E)O(V + E)O(V+E)$, where VVV is the number of vertices and EEE is the number of edges.

2. Breadth-First Search (BFS)

BFS explores all nodes at the present depth level before moving on to nodes at the next depth level. It uses a **queue** to keep track of the nodes to be explored next. BFS is ideal for finding the shortest path in an unweighted graph, as it explores all nodes at one level before moving on to the next.

Steps for BFS:

1. Start from the source node.
2. Visit the node and mark it as visited.
3. Add all unvisited neighbors to the queue.
4. Dequeue a node, visit it, and repeat the process until all nodes are visited.

BFS Implementation:

cpp

```
#include <iostream>
#include <vector>
#include <queue>
using namespace std;

class Graph {
```

```
    int V;
    vector<vector<int>> adjList;

public:
    Graph(int V);
    void addEdge(int u, int v);
    void BFS(int start);
};

Graph::Graph(int V) {
    this->V = V;
    adjList.resize(V);
}

void Graph::addEdge(int u, int v) {
    adjList[u].push_back(v);
}

void Graph::BFS(int start) {
    vector<bool> visited(V, false);
    queue<int> q;

    visited[start] = true;
    q.push(start);

    while (!q.empty()) {
        int node = q.front();
        cout << node << " ";
        q.pop();
```

```
    for (int neighbor : adjList[node]) {
       if (!visited[neighbor]) {
          visited[neighbor] = true;
          q.push(neighbor);
       }
     }
   }
}

int main() {
   Graph g(6);
   g.addEdge(0, 1);
   g.addEdge(0, 2);
   g.addEdge(1, 3);
   g.addEdge(1, 4);
   g.addEdge(2, 5);

   cout << "BFS starting from node 0: ";
   g.BFS(0);

   return 0;
}
```

Explanation:

- The BFS function uses a **queue** to explore nodes level by level.
- Starting from node 0, BFS explores all neighboring nodes before moving to the next level.

- The graph is represented using an adjacency list, and edges are added with the addEdge() function.

Time Complexity: The time complexity of BFS is O(V+E)O(V + E)O(V+E), similar to DFS, where VVV is the number of vertices and EEE is the number of edges.

Real-World Example: Implementing a Web Crawler

A **web crawler** is a program that systematically browses the web to collect data from websites. It is typically implemented using BFS or DFS to explore links (edges) between web pages (nodes).

- In the case of a BFS-based crawler, it would start with a list of URLs to visit (root nodes). It would visit each URL, collect links from that page (edges), and then add those links to the queue for future visits. This process continues until all links are explored.

Steps for a BFS Web Crawler:

1. Start with a list of seed URLs.
2. Add the seed URLs to the queue.
3. Dequeue a URL and retrieve its content.
4. Extract all the hyperlinks (URLs) from the page.
5. Add the new URLs to the queue if they haven't been visited yet.

6. Repeat until all URLs are visited.

Graphs are a fundamental concept in computer science, and mastering graph traversal algorithms like **DFS** and **BFS** is essential for solving many real-world problems, from web crawling to network analysis. Understanding how to represent graphs and implement these basic traversal techniques is the first step towards more complex graph algorithms and problem-solving approaches.

Chapter 11: Advanced Graph Algorithms

In this chapter, we will explore three powerful graph algorithms designed to solve the problem of finding the **shortest path** in weighted graphs: **Dijkstra's Algorithm**, **Bellman-Ford Algorithm**, and the **Floyd-Warshall Algorithm**. These algorithms are used to determine the shortest path between nodes in a graph, and they have applications in various domains like route planning, network routing, and even in recommendation systems.

We'll cover how each of these algorithms works, the key differences between them, and when to use each algorithm based on the problem at hand.

Dijkstra's Algorithm for Shortest Paths

Dijkstra's algorithm is one of the most widely used algorithms for finding the shortest path from a source node to all other nodes in a **weighted graph** with non-negative weights. It is an efficient algorithm that operates in **greedy** fashion, meaning it always selects the nearest unprocessed node at each step.

How Dijkstra's Algorithm Works:

1. Initialize the distance to the source node as 0 and to all other nodes as infinity.
2. Mark all nodes as unvisited.

3. Start from the source node and visit its neighbors, updating their distances if a shorter path is found.

4. Once all neighbors of a node are processed, mark the node as visited.

5. Select the unvisited node with the smallest distance and repeat the process until all nodes are visited.

Steps in the Algorithm:

1. Initialize a distance array with infinity for all nodes except the source.

2. Set the source node's distance to 0.

3. Use a priority queue to efficiently retrieve the node with the smallest distance at each step.

4. For the current node, update the distances to its neighboring nodes if a shorter path is found.

5. Continue the process until all nodes are visited.

Dijkstra's Algorithm Implementation (C++):

cpp

```
#include <iostream>
#include <vector>
#include <queue>
#include <climits>
using namespace std;
```

```cpp
class Graph {
    int V;
    vector<vector<pair<int, int>>> adjList; // adjacency list (pair: node, weight)

public:
    Graph(int V);
    void addEdge(int u, int v, int weight);
    void dijkstra(int start);
};

Graph::Graph(int V) {
    this->V = V;
    adjList.resize(V);
}

void Graph::addEdge(int u, int v, int weight) {
    adjList[u].push_back({v, weight});
    adjList[v].push_back({u, weight}); // for undirected graph
}

void Graph::dijkstra(int start) {
    vector<int> dist(V, INT_MAX);
    dist[start] = 0;

    priority_queue<pair<int, int>, vector<pair<int, int>>, greater<pair<int, int>>> pq;
    pq.push({0, start}); // {distance, node}

    while (!pq.empty()) {
        int node = pq.top().second;
```

```cpp
        int distance = pq.top().first;
        pq.pop();

        // If already processed, skip
        if (distance > dist[node]) continue;

        // Check neighbors
        for (auto& neighbor : adjList[node]) {
            int neighborNode = neighbor.first;
            int edgeWeight = neighbor.second;

            if (dist[node] + edgeWeight < dist[neighborNode]) {
                dist[neighborNode] = dist[node] + edgeWeight;
                pq.push({dist[neighborNode], neighborNode});
            }
        }
    }

    // Output distances
    for (int i = 0; i < V; i++) {
        cout << "Distance from " << start << " to " << i << " is " << dist[i] << endl;
    }
}

int main() {
    Graph g(5);
    g.addEdge(0, 1, 10);
    g.addEdge(0, 2, 5);
    g.addEdge(1, 2, 2);
    g.addEdge(1, 3, 1);
```

```
g.addEdge(2, 3, 9);
g.addEdge(3, 4, 4);

g.dijkstra(0);

return 0;
}
```

Explanation:

- **Graph Representation**: The graph is represented as an adjacency list where each node stores its neighbors along with the edge weights.
- **Priority Queue**: A priority queue (min-heap) is used to efficiently fetch the node with the smallest tentative distance.
- **Time Complexity**: The time complexity is $O(E\log V)O(E \log V)O(E\log V)$, where EEE is the number of edges and VVV is the number of vertices.

Bellman-Ford Algorithm

The **Bellman-Ford algorithm** is similar to Dijkstra's but has a major advantage: it works with **graphs that may contain negative edge weights**. It is slightly less efficient than Dijkstra's algorithm but can handle graphs that Dijkstra's cannot.

How Bellman-Ford Algorithm Works:

1. Initialize the distance to the source node as 0 and to all other nodes as infinity.

2. Relax all edges **V-1 times** (where VVV is the number of vertices), meaning for each edge $u \to v$ u \rightarrow vu→v, if the distance to vvv through uuu is shorter than the current distance, update it.

3. If a negative weight cycle is detected (i.e., an edge can still be relaxed after V−1V-1V−1 iterations), the graph contains a negative weight cycle.

Bellman-Ford Algorithm Implementation (C++):

cpp

```
#include <iostream>
#include <vector>
#include <climits>
using namespace std;

class Graph {
    int V, E;
    vector<tuple<int, int, int>> edges; // (u, v, weight)

public:
    Graph(int V, int E);
    void addEdge(int u, int v, int weight);
    void bellmanFord(int start);
};
```

```cpp
Graph::Graph(int V, int E) {
    this->V = V;
    this->E = E;
}


void Graph::addEdge(int u, int v, int weight) {
    edges.push_back(make_tuple(u, v, weight));
}


void Graph::bellmanFord(int start) {
    vector<int> dist(V, INT_MAX);
    dist[start] = 0;

    // Relax all edges V-1 times
    for (int i = 1; i < V; i++) {
        for (auto& edge : edges) {
            int u, v, weight;
            tie(u, v, weight) = edge;
            if (dist[u] != INT_MAX && dist[u] + weight < dist[v]) {
                dist[v] = dist[u] + weight;
            }
        }
    }

    // Check for negative weight cycle
    for (auto& edge : edges) {
        int u, v, weight;
        tie(u, v, weight) = edge;
        if (dist[u] != INT_MAX && dist[u] + weight < dist[v]) {
            cout << "Graph contains a negative weight cycle." << endl;
```

```
        return;
      }
   }

   // Output distances
   for (int i = 0; i < V; i++) {
      cout << "Distance from " << start << " to " << i << " is " << dist[i] << endl;
   }
}

int main() {
   Graph g(5, 8);
   g.addEdge(0, 1, -1);
   g.addEdge(0, 2, 4);
   g.addEdge(1, 2, 3);
   g.addEdge(1, 3, 2);
   g.addEdge(1, 4, 2);
   g.addEdge(3, 2, 5);
   g.addEdge(3, 1, 1);
   g.addEdge(4, 3, -3);

   g.bellmanFord(0);

   return 0;
}
```

Explanation:

- **Graph Representation**: The graph is represented using a list of edges as tuples (source, destination, weight).

- **Time Complexity**: The time complexity is O(V·E)O(V \cdot E)O(V·E), where VVV is the number of vertices and EEE is the number of edges.

Floyd-Warshall Algorithm

The **Floyd-Warshall algorithm** is an **all-pairs shortest path** algorithm that calculates the shortest paths between all pairs of vertices in a graph. Unlike Dijkstra and Bellman-Ford, which focus on single-source shortest paths, Floyd-Warshall calculates the shortest paths for every pair of nodes, making it useful for dense graphs.

How Floyd-Warshall Algorithm Works:

1. Initialize a distance matrix where dist[i][j]dist[i][j]dist[i][j] is the direct distance from node iii to node jjj. If no edge exists, initialize it to infinity.

2. Update the matrix by iterating over all possible intermediate nodes. For each pair of nodes iii and jjj, check if a path from iii to jjj through an intermediate node kkk is shorter than the direct path from iii to jjj.

3. Repeat for all pairs of nodes and intermediate nodes.

Floyd-Warshall Algorithm Implementation (C++):

cpp

```cpp
#include <iostream>
#include <vector>
#include <climits>
using namespace std;

class Graph {
    int V;
    vector<vector<int>> dist;

public:
    Graph(int V);
    void addEdge(int u, int v, int weight);
    void floydWarshall();
};

Graph::Graph(int V) {
    this->V = V;
    dist.resize(V, vector<int>(V, INT_MAX));
    for (int i = 0; i < V; i++) dist[i][i] = 0;  // Distance to self is 0
}

void Graph::addEdge(int u, int v, int weight) {
    dist[u][v] = weight;
    dist[v][u] = weight;  // For undirected graph
}

void Graph::floydWarshall() {
    for (int k = 0; k < V; k++) {
        for (int i = 0; i < V; i++) {
```

```
        for (int j = 0; j < V; j++) {
            if (dist[i][k] != INT_MAX && dist[k][j] != INT_MAX) {
                dist[i][j] = min(dist[i][j], dist[i][k] + dist[k][j]);
            }
        }
    }
}


    // Output shortest path distances
    for (int i = 0; i < V; i++) {
        for (int j = 0; j < V; j++) {
            cout << "Distance from " << i << " to " << j << " is " << dist[i][j] <<
endl;
        }
    }
}

int main() {
    Graph g(4);
    g.addEdge(0, 1, 5);
    g.addEdge(0, 2, 10);
    g.addEdge(1, 2, 2);
    g.addEdge(1, 3, 1);
    g.addEdge(2, 3, 7);

    g.floydWarshall();

    return 0;
}
```

Explanation:

- **Graph Representation**: The graph is represented as a 2D distance matrix, where the element dist[i][j]dist[i][j]dist[i][j] stores the shortest distance from node iii to node jjj.

- **Time Complexity**: The time complexity is $O(V3)O(V^3)O(V3)$, which makes it less efficient for very large graphs.

Real-World Example: Finding the Shortest Path Between Cities on a Map

In the real world, finding the shortest path between two cities on a map is a common use case for these algorithms. For example, if you are using a map application to plan a route, the app may use Dijkstra's or Floyd-Warshall's algorithm to calculate the quickest route based on road distances and traffic conditions.

In such a map, cities can be represented as nodes, and roads can be represented as edges with weights corresponding to the road length or travel time. The graph algorithms can then be applied to find the shortest route between two cities, or all cities, respectively.

Chapter 12: String Matching Algorithms

String matching is a fundamental problem in computer science that involves finding occurrences of a pattern (or substring) within a text. From simple text searches to complex pattern recognition tasks, string matching algorithms are essential for a wide variety of applications, including search engines, data retrieval, and bioinformatics. In this chapter, we'll cover different approaches to string matching, compare naive and efficient algorithms, and explore the role of regular expressions in solving string matching problems.

We will discuss the following string matching techniques:

1. **Naive String Matching**
2. **Efficient String Matching Algorithms**:
    - **Knuth-Morris-Pratt (KMP) Algorithm**
    - **Rabin-Karp Algorithm**
3. **Regular Expressions and their Applications**
4. **Real-world Example**: Building a search engine for text-based queries.

Naive String Matching Algorithm

The **Naive String Matching Algorithm** is the simplest approach to solving the string matching problem. It works by checking every possible position in the text where the pattern could match. For each position, it checks if the substring starting at that position matches the entire pattern.

How the Naive Algorithm Works:

1. Start at each position in the text and compare the substring starting at that position with the pattern.
2. If a match is found, return the index where the match starts.
3. If no match is found after checking all positions, return that the pattern does not exist in the text.

Time Complexity:

- In the worst case, it takes $O(n \cdot m)O(n \cdot m)O(n \cdot m)$ time where nnn is the length of the text and mmm is the length of the pattern.

Example of Naive Algorithm Implementation (C++):

cpp

```
#include <iostream>
#include <string>
using namespace std;

void naiveStringMatch(const string& text, const string& pattern) {
    int n = text.length();
    int m = pattern.length();
```

```cpp
    for (int i = 0; i <= n - m; i++) {
        int j = 0;
        while (j < m && text[i + j] == pattern[j]) {
            j++;
        }
        if (j == m) {
            cout << "Pattern found at index " << i << endl;
        }
    }
}

int main() {
    string text = "ababcababcab";
    string pattern = "abc";
    naiveStringMatch(text, pattern);
    return 0;
}
```

Explanation:

- The algorithm iterates over every possible position in the text to check for a match with the pattern.
- If a match is found, the starting index is printed.

Knuth-Morris-Pratt (KMP) Algorithm

The **Knuth-Morris-Pratt (KMP) algorithm** is an efficient string matching algorithm that avoids unnecessary re-evaluations of characters that have already been matched. It does so by using information from previous comparisons to skip over sections of the text that cannot match the pattern.

How KMP Works:

1. Preprocess the pattern to create a partial match table (also called the "prefix table").
2. Use this table to avoid redundant checks in the text.

The **prefix table** stores the lengths of the longest proper prefix of the pattern that is also a suffix. For example, for the pattern "ABAB", the longest prefix that is also a suffix is "AB", so the prefix table would store the value 2 for this pattern.

Steps in KMP Algorithm:

1. Preprocess the pattern to build the prefix table.
2. Use the table to skip over unmatched characters in the text.

Time Complexity:

- **Preprocessing**: $O(m)O(m)O(m)$, where mmm is the length of the pattern.
- **Matching**: $O(n)O(n)O(n)$, where nnn is the length of the text.

KMP Algorithm Implementation (C++):

cpp

```cpp
#include <iostream>
#include <vector>
#include <string>
using namespace std;

// Preprocess the pattern to create the prefix table
vector<int> buildPrefixTable(const string& pattern) {
    int m = pattern.length();
    vector<int> prefixTable(m, 0);
    int j = 0;

    for (int i = 1; i < m; i++) {
        while (j > 0 && pattern[i] != pattern[j]) {
            j = prefixTable[j - 1];
        }
        if (pattern[i] == pattern[j]) {
            j++;
        }
        prefixTable[i] = j;
    }

    return prefixTable;
}

// KMP algorithm for string matching
void kmpStringMatch(const string& text, const string& pattern) {
    int n = text.length();
    int m = pattern.length();
```

```
vector<int> prefixTable = buildPrefixTable(pattern);
int j = 0;  // Index for pattern

for (int i = 0; i < n; i++) {
    while (j > 0 && text[i] != pattern[j]) {
        j = prefixTable[j - 1];  // Skip redundant matches
    }
    if (text[i] == pattern[j]) {
        j++;
    }
    if (j == m) {
        cout << "Pattern found at index " << i - m + 1 << endl;
        j = prefixTable[j - 1];  // Continue searching for next match
    }
}
}

int main() {
    string text = "ababcababcab";
    string pattern = "abc";
    kmpStringMatch(text, pattern);
    return 0;
}
```

Explanation:

- The **prefix table** is built for the pattern before the actual matching begins.

- As we traverse the text, we use the prefix table to avoid re-checking previously matched characters, making the algorithm more efficient.

Rabin-Karp Algorithm

The **Rabin-Karp Algorithm** uses hashing to quickly identify potential matches for a pattern in a text. Instead of checking each character one by one, it computes a hash value for the pattern and the substrings of the text and compares the hash values. If the hash values match, it then checks the actual characters to confirm the match.

How Rabin-Karp Works:

1. Compute the hash of the pattern and the first substring of the text.
2. Compare the hashes. If they match, check the characters of the text and pattern.
3. Slide the window over the text, compute the hash of the next substring, and repeat the process.

Time Complexity:

- In the average case, the time complexity is $O(n+m)O(n + m)O(n+m)$, where nnn is the length of the text and mmm is the length of the pattern. In the worst case, it's O(n·m)O(n \cdot m)O(n·m) due to hash collisions.

Rabin-Karp Algorithm Implementation (C++):

cpp

```
#include <iostream>
#include <string>
#include <cmath>
using namespace std;

const int d = 256;  // Number of characters in the alphabet (ASCII)
const int q = 101;  // A prime number for modulus

void rabinKarpStringMatch(const string& text, const string& pattern) {
    int n = text.length();
    int m = pattern.length();
    int i, j;
    int patternHash = 0;  // Hash of the pattern
    int textHash = 0;     // Hash of the text
    int h = 1;

    // Calculate the value of h (d^(m-1) % q)
    for (i = 0; i < m - 1; i++) {
        h = (h * d) % q;
    }

    // Calculate initial hash values for the pattern and the first window of text
    for (i = 0; i < m; i++) {
```

MASTERING ALGORITHMS WITH C++


```cpp
        patternHash = (d * patternHash + pattern[i]) % q;
        textHash = (d * textHash + text[i]) % q;
    }


    // Slide the pattern over the text
    for (i = 0; i <= n - m; i++) {
        // Check if hash values match
        if (patternHash == textHash) {
            for (j = 0; j < m; j++) {
                if (text[i + j] != pattern[j]) {
                    break;
                }
            }
            if (j == m) {
                cout << "Pattern found at index " << i << endl;
            }
        }


        // Calculate hash for the next window of text
        if (i < n - m) {
            textHash = (d * (textHash - text[i] * h) + text[i + m]) % q;
            if (textHash < 0) {
                textHash = (textHash + q);
            }
        }
    }
}


int main() {
    string text = "ababcababcab";
```

```
string pattern = "abc";
rabinKarpStringMatch(text, pattern);
return 0;
}
```

Explanation:

- The algorithm computes hash values for both the pattern and text substrings.
- Hash collisions are handled by checking the actual characters if the hashes match.
- This approach allows faster matching when the hash values are used efficiently.

Regular Expressions and Their Applications

Regular expressions (regex) are sequences of characters that define a search pattern. They are used for pattern matching within strings. In string matching algorithms, regex provides a flexible and powerful way to search, extract, and manipulate strings based on specific patterns.

Some common applications of regular expressions include:

- **Text search and replace**: Searching for a pattern and replacing it with a new string.
- **Data validation**: Ensuring that input data matches a specific format, such as email addresses or phone numbers.

- **Text processing**: Extracting useful data from large volumes of unstructured text, such as log files or documents.

For example, using regex, you can match an email address in a body of text with the pattern \w+@\w+\.\w+.

Real-World Example: Building a Search Engine for Text-Based Queries

One of the most common applications of string matching algorithms is in search engines, where users input a query and the system matches relevant documents based on the query string. A search engine needs to process large amounts of text quickly and efficiently, and algorithms like KMP or Rabin-Karp can be used to perform fast text matching.

In such systems:

- **Text matching** is used to identify documents that contain the query words.
- **Ranking** is used to return the most relevant results based on other factors such as keyword frequency, document relevance, and user feedback.

- **Regular expressions** can be used to enhance search features, like handling wildcard queries or finding patterns in the text.

For example, consider a search engine that allows users to search for books by title, author, or genre. The backend could use string matching algorithms to search through a database of book records, providing results in a fraction of a second. Regular expressions can further enhance the functionality, allowing for more complex searches like wildcard searches or pattern matching (e.g., searching for authors whose name starts with "J").

In this chapter, we've explored several important string matching algorithms: Naive, KMP, Rabin-Karp, and Regular Expressions. Each has its strengths and weaknesses, depending on the use case. By understanding how they work, you can select the most appropriate algorithm for your problem and implement efficient text-based systems like search engines or pattern recognition tools.

Chapter 13: Network Flow Algorithms

Network flow algorithms are crucial in solving problems that involve the transportation or distribution of resources through a network, such as maximizing the flow of goods, services, or information through a system. These algorithms have applications in fields ranging from telecommunications and traffic management to supply chain logistics and operations research.

In this chapter, we will explore **flow networks**, **the maximum flow problem**, and dive into two well-known algorithms used to solve this problem: the **Ford-Fulkerson algorithm** and the **Edmonds-Karp algorithm**. We will also explore a real-world example of solving a **network flow problem**, such as optimizing traffic management in a city.

What is a Flow Network?
A **flow network** is a directed graph where:

- Each edge has a **capacity** (a limit on the flow that can pass through it).
- Each edge carries a **flow**, which represents the quantity of the resource (e.g., traffic, data, goods) passing from one node to another.
- The graph has a **source node** from which the flow starts and a **sink node** where the flow ends.

The **maximum flow problem** involves finding the greatest possible flow from the source node to the sink node, subject to the capacities on the edges. This is a typical optimization problem in various applications, including network routing, transportation systems, and supply chain management.

The Max Flow Problem

The **max flow problem** asks: *How can we maximize the flow from the source node to the sink node in a network, subject to edge capacity constraints?*

The solution is often based on finding paths through the graph where additional flow can be pushed from the source to the sink, and then repeatedly augmenting the flow until no more augmenting paths exist. The capacity constraints ensure that the flow cannot exceed the limits of each edge.

In general, the max flow problem can be formulated as follows:

- **Input**: A directed graph with source and sink nodes, and capacity values on each edge.
- **Output**: The maximum flow from the source to the sink.

To solve this, several algorithms have been developed, two of the most prominent being the **Ford-Fulkerson** algorithm and the **Edmonds-Karp** algorithm.

Ford-Fulkerson Algorithm

The **Ford-Fulkerson algorithm** is a greedy method for computing the maximum flow in a flow network. The main idea is to repeatedly find an augmenting path (a path from source to sink where additional flow can be pushed) and increase the flow along that path. This process continues until no more augmenting paths can be found.

Steps in Ford-Fulkerson Algorithm:

1. **Initialization**: Set the flow of all edges to 0.
2. **Find Augmenting Path**: Search for a path from the source to the sink where the flow can be increased. The path must respect the edge capacities (i.e., no edge can carry more flow than its capacity).
3. **Augment Flow**: Once an augmenting path is found, increase the flow along that path by the smallest available capacity along the path.
4. **Update Residual Graph**: After augmenting the flow, update the residual graph by subtracting the flow added along each edge and increasing the reverse flow.
5. **Repeat**: Repeat steps 2 to 4 until no more augmenting paths can be found.

Time Complexity: In the worst case, Ford-Fulkerson can take an exponential amount of time (since it might repeatedly find augmenting paths in an inefficient manner). However, for networks with integer capacities, it will terminate in polynomial time.

Example (C++ Implementation):

cpp

```cpp
#include <iostream>
#include <vector>
#include <queue>
#include <climits>
using namespace std;

class Graph {
public:
    int V;
    vector<vector<int>> capacity, flow;

    Graph(int V) {
        this->V = V;
        capacity.assign(V, vector<int>(V, 0));
        flow.assign(V, vector<int>(V, 0));
    }

    void addEdge(int u, int v, int cap) {
        capacity[u][v] = cap;
    }
```

```cpp
int bfs(int source, int sink, vector<int>& parent) {
    vector<bool> visited(V, false);
    queue<int> q;
    q.push(source);
    visited[source] = true;
    parent[source] = -1;

    while (!q.empty()) {
        int u = q.front();
        q.pop();

        for (int v = 0; v < V; v++) {
            if (!visited[v] && capacity[u][v] - flow[u][v] > 0) {
                q.push(v);
                visited[v] = true;
                parent[v] = u;

                if (v == sink) {
                    return true;
                }
            }
        }
    }
    return false;
}

int fordFulkerson(int source, int sink) {
    vector<int> parent(V, -1);
    int maxFlow = 0;
```

```
        while (bfs(source, sink, parent)) {
            int pathFlow = INT_MAX;
            for (int v = sink; v != source; v = parent[v]) {
                int u = parent[v];
                pathFlow = min(pathFlow, capacity[u][v] - flow[u][v]);
            }

            for (int v = sink; v != source; v = parent[v]) {
                int u = parent[v];
                flow[u][v] += pathFlow;
                flow[v][u] -= pathFlow;
            }

            maxFlow += pathFlow;
        }
        return maxFlow;
    }
};

int main() {
    Graph g(6);
    g.addEdge(0, 1, 16);
    g.addEdge(0, 2, 13);
    g.addEdge(1, 2, 10);
    g.addEdge(1, 3, 12);
    g.addEdge(2, 1, 4);
    g.addEdge(2, 4, 14);
    g.addEdge(3, 2, 9);
    g.addEdge(3, 5, 20);
    g.addEdge(4, 3, 7);
```

```
g.addEdge(4, 5, 4);

cout << "Maximum Flow: " << g.fordFulkerson(0, 5) << endl;

return 0;
}
```

Explanation:

- In this implementation, we build a graph with edge capacities, and then use BFS to find augmenting paths from the source to the sink. The flow is updated along the path, and the process continues until no more augmenting paths are found.

Edmonds-Karp Algorithm

The **Edmonds-Karp algorithm** is an implementation of the Ford-Fulkerson method that uses **Breadth-First Search (BFS)** to find augmenting paths. The key improvement is that BFS ensures that the shortest augmenting path (in terms of the number of edges) is chosen, which guarantees that the algorithm runs in polynomial time.

Key Difference from Ford-Fulkerson:

- Ford-Fulkerson can use any method to find augmenting paths, whereas Edmonds-Karp specifically uses BFS to guarantee polynomial time performance.

Time Complexity:

- The time complexity of the Edmonds-Karp algorithm is $O(V \times E^2)$, where V is the number of vertices and E is the number of edges. This is significantly more efficient than the basic Ford-Fulkerson algorithm.

Real-World Example: Traffic Management

A **real-world application** of network flow algorithms is in traffic management systems. Imagine a city with several intersections connected by roads, and each road has a maximum traffic capacity (number of cars it can handle per hour). The goal is to maximize the flow of traffic from a starting point (e.g., a highway entrance) to an endpoint (e.g., a downtown area), while ensuring that no road exceeds its capacity.

By modeling the city's road network as a flow network, we can apply the **max flow algorithms** to optimize the flow of traffic. The source represents the entrance points of vehicles into the city, and the sink represents the final destination. Each road's capacity can be set based on the maximum cars that can travel on that road in an hour. The algorithms will determine the maximum number of cars that can flow through the network while respecting the road capacities.

For example, the Ford-Fulkerson or Edmonds-Karp algorithm could be used to adjust traffic signals or route traffic in a way that maximizes the number of cars reaching their destination without overloading any single road.

In this chapter, we've explored the theory behind **network flow algorithms**, focusing on the **Ford-Fulkerson** and **Edmonds-Karp** algorithms for solving the **maximum flow problem**. Through the application of these algorithms, we can optimize resources in various scenarios such as traffic management, data flow in networks, and logistics. Understanding how to approach flow problems is critical in designing efficient and scalable systems for real-world applications.

Chapter 14: Computational Geometry Algorithms

Computational geometry is a field of computer science and mathematics that deals with the study of algorithms for solving geometric problems. These problems typically involve points, lines, shapes, and the relationships between them. Computational geometry plays a crucial role in applications such as computer graphics, computer-aided design (CAD), robotics, geographic information systems (GIS), and more.

In this chapter, we will dive into **computational geometry algorithms** that address common geometric problems. We will cover **convex hulls**, **line segment intersection**, and the **closest pair problem**. Finally, we will look at a **real-world example** of how these algorithms can be applied in **pathfinding** for robots or autonomous vehicles.

What is Computational Geometry?
Computational geometry involves the design and analysis of algorithms that solve geometric problems. These problems involve sets of points, lines, curves, and other geometric objects, and the goal is to solve problems that arise when dealing with geometric objects in an efficient manner.

For example, problems in computational geometry may involve:

- Finding the intersection of two lines.
- Determining whether a point is inside a polygon.
- Finding the shortest path between two points in a plane.

The key challenges in computational geometry include:

- **Efficiency**: Some geometric problems can have complex solutions, and solving them efficiently (in terms of time and space) is critical.
- **Accuracy**: Geometric algorithms need to handle real-world precision issues, especially in applications like computer graphics, robotics, and CAD.

Convex Hull Algorithms

The **convex hull** of a set of points is the smallest convex polygon (or polyhedron in 3D) that contains all of the points. In simpler terms, it's like stretching a rubber band around a set of points and seeing the shape it forms. The convex hull is a fundamental concept in computational geometry and is used in various applications like pattern recognition, image processing, and robotics.

- **Use Case**: Finding the convex hull of a set of points can be helpful for problems like collision detection, where you want to check if two convex shapes are intersecting.
- **Algorithm Overview**: The most well-known algorithm for finding the convex hull is **Graham's scan**, which operates in $O(n\log n)$ $O(n \log n)$ $O(nlogn)$ time. Another popular algorithm is **Jarvis' march**, also known as the gift wrapping algorithm, which runs in $O(nh)$ $O(nh)$ $O(nh)$, where h is the number of points on the convex hull.

Graham's Scan Algorithm (Step-by-step):

1. **Find the pivot**: Choose the point with the lowest y-coordinate (and lowest x-coordinate in case of ties).
2. **Sort the points**: Sort the remaining points by the angle they make with the pivot.
3. **Construct the hull**: Start with the pivot and iterate through the sorted points, adding them to the hull if they turn counterclockwise. If a clockwise turn is detected, backtrack and remove the last point added.

Code Example (C++):

cpp

```
#include <iostream>
#include <vector>
```

141

```cpp
#include <algorithm>
using namespace std;

struct Point {
    int x, y;
};

// Function to compare two points
bool compare(Point p1, Point p2) {
    return (p1.x < p2.x) || (p1.x == p2.x && p1.y < p2.y);
}

// Cross product to check orientation
int crossProduct(Point p1, Point p2, Point p3) {
    return (p2.x - p1.x) * (p3.y - p1.y) - (p2.y - p1.y) * (p3.x - p1.x);
}

vector<Point> convexHull(vector<Point>& points) {
    sort(points.begin(), points.end(), compare);

    vector<Point> hull;

    // Build lower hull
    for (Point p : points) {
        while (hull.size() >= 2 && crossProduct(hull[hull.size() - 2], hull.back(), p) <= 0) {
            hull.pop_back();
        }
        hull.push_back(p);
    }
```

```
// Build upper hull
int t = hull.size() + 1;
for (int i = points.size() - 1; i >= 0; i--) {
    while (hull.size() >= t && crossProduct(hull[hull.size() - 2], hull.back(),
points[i]) <= 0) {
        hull.pop_back();
    }
    hull.push_back(points[i]);
}

hull.pop_back(); // Remove the last point which is repeated

return hull;
}

int main() {
    vector<Point> points = {{0, 0}, {1, 1}, {2, 2}, {2, 0}, {3, 1}, {3, 3}, {0, 3}};
    vector<Point> result = convexHull(points);

    cout << "Convex Hull: ";
    for (Point p : result) {
        cout << "(" << p.x << ", " << p.y << ") ";
    }
    return 0;
}
```

Line Segment Intersection

The **line segment intersection problem** is a fundamental problem in computational geometry, where we want to determine if two line segments intersect. This problem arises in various fields, including computer graphics, CAD, and robotics, where determining intersections between objects is crucial for tasks such as collision detection.

- **Algorithm Overview**: A common approach to solving this problem is using **sweep line algorithms**. These algorithms involve sweeping a vertical line from left to right, maintaining an ordered list of active line segments that intersect the sweep line. When the sweep line moves across a new event, the algorithm checks for potential intersections between active segments.

Steps for Line Segment Intersection:

1. **Sort the events**: Events include the left and right endpoints of the line segments.
2. **Process events**: As the sweep line moves across events, check for intersections between the active segments.
3. **Detect intersection**: If two segments cross each other, they intersect, and their intersection point can be calculated.

Use Case: This algorithm is widely used in computer graphics to detect when objects overlap, and in geographical information systems (GIS) to analyze spatial data.

Closest Pair of Points Problem

The **closest pair of points problem** involves finding the two points in a set of points that are closest to each other. This is a fundamental problem in computational geometry with applications in fields like clustering, pattern recognition, and geographical analysis.

- **Algorithm Overview**: A brute-force solution would check all pairs of points, which takes $O(n^2)$ time. However, a more efficient algorithm is based on **divide and conquer** and works in $O(n \log n)$ time. The basic idea is to recursively divide the set of points into two halves, find the closest pairs in each half, and then check for potential closer pairs across the dividing line.

Steps for Closest Pair of Points:

1. **Sort the points**: Sort the points based on their x-coordinates.
2. **Divide and conquer**: Recursively divide the points into two halves and find the closest pairs within each half.
3. **Merge step**: During the merge step, check for potential closest pairs that lie near the dividing line.

Real-World Example: Pathfinding for Robots or Autonomous Vehicles

One of the most exciting applications of computational geometry is in **pathfinding for robots or autonomous vehicles**. Pathfinding involves finding a route from one point to another, typically avoiding obstacles. Many of the problems in robotics and autonomous vehicles, such as collision detection, map navigation, and motion planning, are deeply rooted in computational geometry.

For example, when designing a robot that navigates through a maze, algorithms like **convex hull** can be used to calculate the boundary of obstacles, and **line segment intersection** algorithms help detect collisions with walls or other obstacles. The **closest pair of points** problem can be used to find the nearest objects to the robot, which is crucial for navigating through tight spaces.

By applying computational geometry algorithms, we can efficiently calculate the best paths for robots or autonomous vehicles, enabling them to make real-time decisions in dynamic environments.

In this chapter, we have explored some of the core problems in **computational geometry** and discussed algorithms like **convex**

hull, **line segment intersection**, and the **closest pair of points** problem. These algorithms have wide-ranging applications, from robotics and computer graphics to GIS and CAD. Understanding and mastering these algorithms will provide you with the tools to solve complex geometric problems efficiently and accurately. In the real world, computational geometry plays an essential role in enabling systems to navigate, interact with, and understand the physical world.

Chapter 15: String Algorithms

Strings are fundamental data types in computer science, used to represent text. Efficient manipulation and processing of strings are crucial for tasks such as searching, pattern matching, text analysis, and even building applications like search engines or autocomplete features. In this chapter, we will explore advanced string algorithms, focusing on **efficient string manipulation**, **suffix arrays**, and **tries**. We'll also look at real-world applications of these techniques, including **text analysis** and **autocomplete features**.

Efficient String Manipulation and Matching Techniques

String manipulation is a critical part of many algorithms, and understanding how to optimize these operations can make a huge difference in performance. Some of the most common tasks include:

- **Searching for a substring**: Finding whether a string contains another substring.
- **Pattern matching**: Identifying occurrences of a pattern within a text string.
- **String comparison**: Comparing two strings to check for equality or lexicographic order.

Naive String Matching

The **naive string matching** algorithm involves checking for the substring at every position in the string. For a string of length nnn and a pattern of length mmm, the naive approach performs $O(n×m)O(n \times m)O(n×m)$ comparisons, making it inefficient for large inputs.

Example: For a text "hello world" and the pattern "world", the naive algorithm checks each possible position in the text to see if the substring matches the pattern.

Knuth-Morris-Pratt (KMP) Algorithm

The **KMP algorithm** is an efficient string matching algorithm that preprocesses the pattern to create a partial match table (also known as the **prefix function**). This table allows the algorithm to skip unnecessary comparisons, reducing the worst-case time complexity to $O(n+m)O(n + m)O(n+m)$, where nnn is the length of the text and mmm is the length of the pattern.

The KMP algorithm avoids redundant comparisons by using information from previous matches. The idea is that if a mismatch occurs at position iii, we use the prefix function to skip to the next potential match.

Code Example (C++):

cpp

```cpp
#include <iostream>
#include <vector>
using namespace std;

// Compute the prefix function (partial match table)
vector<int> computePrefixFunction(const string& pattern) {
    int m = pattern.size();
    vector<int> prefixFunction(m, 0);
    int j = 0;

    for (int i = 1; i < m; ++i) {
        while (j > 0 && pattern[i] != pattern[j]) {
            j = prefixFunction[j - 1];
        }
        if (pattern[i] == pattern[j]) {
            ++j;
        }
        prefixFunction[i] = j;
    }

    return prefixFunction;
}

// KMP algorithm for pattern matching
vector<int> KMPSearch(const string& text, const string& pattern) {
    vector<int> result;
    int n = text.size();
    int m = pattern.size();

    vector<int> prefixFunction = computePrefixFunction(pattern);
```

```
    int j = 0; // Index for pattern
    for (int i = 0; i < n; ++i) {
        while (j > 0 && text[i] != pattern[j]) {
            j = prefixFunction[j - 1];
        }

        if (text[i] == pattern[j]) {
            ++j;
        }

        if (j == m) {
            result.push_back(i - m + 1); // Match found at index (i - m + 1)
            j = prefixFunction[j - 1];
        }
    }

    return result;
}

int main() {
    string text = "ababcababcabc";
    string pattern = "abc";

    vector<int> result = KMPSearch(text, pattern);

    cout << "Pattern found at indices: ";
    for (int index : result) {
        cout << index << " ";
    }
```

```
    return 0;
}
```

Suffix Arrays and Their Applications

A **suffix array** is a data structure that represents all the suffixes of a given string in lexicographical order. It is often used in string matching, data compression, and bioinformatics. The suffix array allows us to perform efficient substring searches and other string operations with better time complexity than traditional methods.

Constructing a Suffix Array

A suffix array can be constructed in $O(n\log n)O(n \log n)O(nlogn)$ time, where nnn is the length of the string. The idea is to sort all the suffixes of the string and store their starting indices.

Steps for constructing a suffix array:

1. **Generate all suffixes** of the string.
2. **Sort** the suffixes lexicographically.
3. **Store the starting indices** of the sorted suffixes.

For example, for the string "banana", the suffixes are:

- "banana"
- "anana"
- "nana"
- "ana"
- "na"

- "a"

After sorting them lexicographically, we get the suffix array, which stores the starting indices of the sorted suffixes.

Suffix Array and LCP Array

A **longest common prefix (LCP)** array can be constructed alongside the suffix array. The LCP array stores the lengths of the longest common prefixes between consecutive suffixes in the sorted order. The combination of the suffix array and the LCP array can be used to perform fast substring searches and find repeated patterns efficiently.

Real-World Example: In bioinformatics, suffix arrays are used for **genome sequence matching**, where rapid searching for substrings in large DNA sequences is necessary.

Code Example (C++):

cpp

```
#include <iostream>
#include <vector>
#include <algorithm>
using namespace std;

// Suffix Array construction using O(n log n) approach
vector<int> buildSuffixArray(const string& str) {
    int n = str.size();
    vector<int> suffixArray(n), rank(n), tempRank(n);
```

```cpp
    for (int i = 0; i < n; ++i) {
        suffixArray[i] = i;
        rank[i] = str[i];
    }

    for (int len = 1; len < n; len *= 2) {
        auto compare = [&rank, &len, n](int i, int j) {
            if (rank[i] != rank[j]) return rank[i] < rank[j];
            int ri = i + len < n ? rank[i + len] : -1;
            int rj = j + len < n ? rank[j + len] : -1;
            return ri < rj;
        };

        sort(suffixArray.begin(), suffixArray.end(), compare);

        tempRank[suffixArray[0]] = 0;
        for (int i = 1; i < n; ++i) {
            tempRank[suffixArray[i]] = tempRank[suffixArray[i - 1]];
            if (compare(suffixArray[i - 1], suffixArray[i])) {
                tempRank[suffixArray[i]]++;
            }
        }
        rank = tempRank;
    }

    return suffixArray;
}

int main() {
```

```
string str = "banana";
vector<int> suffixArray = buildSuffixArray(str);

cout << "Suffix Array: ";
for (int i : suffixArray) {
    cout << i << " ";
}
return 0;
}
```

Tries: A Powerful Data Structure for Strings

A **trie** (pronounced "try") is a tree-like data structure that is used to efficiently store a set of strings. Each node in a trie represents a single character, and the path from the root to a leaf node represents a complete string. Tries are particularly useful for operations like **prefix matching**, **autocomplete**, and **dictionary lookups**.

Applications of Tries

- **Autocomplete**: Tries can quickly find all words that start with a given prefix. This is useful in search engines and text editors.
- **Spell Checking**: Tries can be used to store a dictionary and efficiently check if a word is valid.
- **IP Routing**: In networking, tries can be used to perform fast IP address lookups.

Trie Operations

- **Insertion**: To insert a word into a trie, we start at the root and insert each character of the word, creating new nodes as necessary.

- **Search**: To search for a word, we follow the path from the root to the leaf node corresponding to the word. If any character is missing along the path, the word doesn't exist in the trie.

Code Example (C++):

cpp

```cpp
#include <iostream>
#include <unordered_map>
using namespace std;

class TrieNode {
public:
    unordered_map<char, TrieNode*> children;
    bool isEndOfWord;

    TrieNode() : isEndOfWord(false) {}
};

class Trie {
private:
    TrieNode* root;
```

```cpp
public:
  Trie() {
    root = new TrieNode();
  }

  void insert(const string& word) {
    TrieNode* current = root;
    for (char c : word) {
      if (current->children.find(c) == current->children.end()) {
        current->children[c] = new TrieNode();
      }
      current = current->children[c];
    }
    current->isEndOfWord = true;
  }

  bool search(const string& word) {
    TrieNode* current = root;
    for (char c : word) {
      if (current->children.find(c) == current->children.end()) {
        return false;
      }
      current = current->children[c];
    }
    return current->isEndOfWord;
  }
};

int main() {
```

```
Trie trie;
trie.insert("apple");
trie.insert("app");

cout << "Search 'apple': " << trie.search("apple") << endl;
cout << "Search 'app': " << trie.search("app") << endl;
cout << "Search 'appl': " << trie.search("appl") << endl;

return 0;
}
```

Real-World Example: Text Analysis and Autocomplete Features

String algorithms such as **KMP, suffix arrays**, and **tries** are widely used in various real-world applications, including:

1. **Text Analysis**: Algorithms like KMP and suffix arrays are used in text analysis tools to search for keywords, perform pattern matching, or analyze large volumes of textual data efficiently.

2. **Autocomplete**: Tries are commonly used to implement autocomplete systems in search engines, word processors, and mobile devices. As the user types a query, the system quickly finds all words in the trie that match the typed prefix, offering suggestions in real-time.

In this chapter, we explored the world of string algorithms, covering techniques like **KMP, suffix arrays**, and **tries**. These powerful data structures and algorithms enable efficient string manipulation, pattern matching, and real-time applications such as **autocomplete** and **text analysis**. By mastering these techniques, you can solve complex problems in areas ranging from search engines to bioinformatics, and more.

Chapter 16: Disjoint Set Union (Union-Find)

The **Disjoint Set Union (DSU)**, also known as **Union-Find**, is a powerful data structure that helps in efficiently managing a collection of disjoint sets. It supports two primary operations:

1. **Find**: Determines the root of the set to which an element belongs.
2. **Union**: Merges two sets into one.

This data structure is especially useful for solving problems related to **connected components** and is commonly used in **graph algorithms**. In this chapter, we will dive into how the union-find data structure works, its applications in algorithms like **Kruskal's algorithm**, and how it can be applied in real-world problems such as **social network connectivity**.

Understanding the Union-Find Data Structure
The union-find data structure manages a collection of **disjoint sets**. Each set represents a group of elements, and the union-find structure supports the following operations:

- **Find (x)**: This operation returns the representative (or root) of the set containing element x. It helps to determine whether two elements belong to the same set.
- **Union (x, y)**: This operation merges the sets containing elements x and y into a single set.

The **key idea** behind union-find is to store each set as a **tree**, where each element points to a "parent," and the root of the tree represents the set.

Key Concepts in Union-Find

- **Path Compression**: When performing the Find operation, we make the tree flatter by pointing each node directly to the root. This optimization ensures that future Find operations are faster.
- **Union by Rank/Size**: When performing the Union operation, we attach the smaller tree to the root of the larger tree to keep the tree balanced. This minimizes the tree height and improves efficiency.

Union-Find Operations with Optimizations

The combination of **path compression** and **union by rank** (or size) ensures that the Find and Union operations have near-constant time complexity. In fact, with these optimizations, the time complexity of each operation is $O(\alpha(n))$$O(\alpha(n))$$O(\alpha(n))$, where α\alpha$\alpha$ is the **inverse Ackermann function**, which grows extremely slowly, making it nearly constant in practical terms.

Code Example (C++):

cpp

```cpp
#include <iostream>
#include <vector>
using namespace std;

class UnionFind {
private:
  vector<int> parent, rank;

public:
  // Constructor to initialize the data structure
  UnionFind(int size) {
    parent.resize(size);
    rank.resize(size, 0);
    for (int i = 0; i < size; ++i) {
      parent[i] = i; // Initially, each element is its own parent
    }
  }

  // Find the representative (root) of the set containing x
  int find(int x) {
    if (parent[x] != x) {
      parent[x] = find(parent[x]); // Path compression
    }
    return parent[x];
```

```
    }


    // Union of the sets containing x and y
    void unionSets(int x, int y) {
        int rootX = find(x);
        int rootY = find(y);

        if (rootX != rootY) {
            // Union by rank: attach the tree with lower rank to the tree with higher
rank
            if (rank[rootX] > rank[rootY]) {
                parent[rootY] = rootX;
            } else if (rank[rootX] < rank[rootY]) {
                parent[rootX] = rootY;
            } else {
                parent[rootY] = rootX;
                rank[rootX]++;
            }
        }
    }
};

int main() {
    UnionFind uf(10);

    // Perform some union operations
    uf.unionSets(1, 2);
    uf.unionSets(2, 3);
    uf.unionSets(4, 5);
```

```
// Check if two elements are connected
cout << "1 and 3 are in the same set? " << (uf.find(1) == uf.find(3) ? "Yes" :
"No") << endl;
    cout << "1 and 4 are in the same set? " << (uf.find(1) == uf.find(4) ? "Yes" :
"No") << endl;

    return 0;
}
```

Applications of Union-Find

The Union-Find data structure is widely used in various graph algorithms and problems that deal with **connected components**. Some prominent applications include:

1. Kruskal's Algorithm (Minimum Spanning Tree)

Kruskal's algorithm is a **greedy algorithm** used to find the minimum spanning tree (MST) of a graph. The algorithm involves sorting all edges by weight and then adding edges to the MST one by one, ensuring that no cycles are formed. The Union-Find data structure is crucial in this algorithm for efficiently checking whether two vertices are in the same connected component (i.e., whether adding an edge would create a cycle).

- **Union**: Merge the sets (components) of the two vertices connected by the edge.
- **Find**: Check if the two vertices are already connected (i.e., if they belong to the same set).

By using Union-Find, Kruskal's algorithm runs in $O(E\log E)O(E$ \log E)O(ElogE) time, where EEE is the number of edges in the graph.

Real-World Example: In a **network of cities**, Kruskal's algorithm can be used to design the minimum-cost road network connecting all cities without forming loops.

2. Connected Components in Graphs

In an undirected graph, the goal is often to find the **connected components** — groups of vertices where each vertex is reachable from any other vertex in the same group. The Union-Find data structure is ideal for this problem because it can efficiently track and merge sets of connected vertices.

For example, in a **social network**, you may want to find which groups of people are connected based on mutual friendships. The Union-Find structure allows us to keep track of these connections efficiently.

Real-World Example: Implementing Social Network Connectivity

Consider a **social network** where users can form friendships. The goal is to determine if two users are part of the same social group. This is a classic **connected components** problem.

For instance, let's say we have the following friendships:

- Alice is friends with Bob.
- Bob is friends with Charlie.
- David is friends with Eve.
- Alice is not friends with David.

We want to find out whether Alice and David are part of the same group.

By using the Union-Find data structure, we can perform the following operations:

1. **Union(Alice, Bob)** – Alice and Bob are in the same group.
2. **Union(Bob, Charlie)** – Alice, Bob, and Charlie are in the same group.
3. **Union(David, Eve)** – David and Eve form a different group.

Finally, we check if Alice and David are in the same group using the find operation. Since Alice and Bob are in the same group, and Bob and Charlie are in the same group, Alice, Bob, and Charlie are in one group. However, David and Eve are in a separate group, so the answer is "No."

Code Example (C++):

cpp

```
int main() {
    UnionFind uf(6);  // Let's assume 6 users: Alice, Bob, Charlie, David, Eve,
and Frank

    // Friendship relations
    uf.unionSets(0, 1);  // Alice is friends with Bob
    uf.unionSets(1, 2);  // Bob is friends with Charlie
    uf.unionSets(3, 4);  // David is friends with Eve

    // Check if Alice and David are in the same group
    cout << "Are Alice and David in the same group? "
         << (uf.find(0) == uf.find(3) ? "Yes" : "No") << endl;

    return 0;
}
```

The **Union-Find (Disjoint Set Union)** data structure is a powerful and efficient tool for managing sets and determining the connectivity between elements. With its applications in algorithms like **Kruskal's Minimum Spanning Tree**, **connected components**, and **social network analysis**, the union-find structure is widely used in computer science and real-world applications.

Through optimizations like **path compression** and **union by rank**, Union-Find allows for nearly constant-time operations, making it an indispensable tool for efficiently solving problems in graph theory, networking, and beyond.

Chapter 17: Advanced Search Algorithms

In this chapter, we will explore **advanced search algorithms** used to efficiently find optimal paths in complex problem spaces. These algorithms go beyond the basic search methods like **Breadth-First Search (BFS)** and **Depth-First Search (DFS)**, providing faster solutions and optimizations, especially for pathfinding problems. We will cover the *A (A-star)** search algorithm, **Bidirectional Search**, and *IDA (Iterative Deepening A)***, along with their real-world applications.

---

*Introduction to the A Search Algorithm**

The *A (A-star)** search algorithm is one of the most popular and efficient algorithms for finding the shortest path between nodes in a graph. It is widely used in applications like **robot navigation**, **game AI**, and **map-based routing systems**. The key advantage of A* over other search algorithms is its ability to use both **path cost** and **heuristic estimates** to find the optimal path quickly.

The A* algorithm uses a combination of two functions to evaluate each node:

1. **g(n)**: The actual cost from the starting node to node n (i.e., the path already traveled).

MASTERING ALGORITHMS WITH C++

2. **h(n)**: The heuristic estimate of the cost from node n to the goal node (i.e., an educated guess).

The sum of these functions gives the total cost of reaching the goal through node n:

$$f(n)=g(n)+h(n)f(n) = g(n) + h(n)f(n)=g(n)+h(n)$$

Where:

- **g(n)** is the cost to get from the start node to n.
- **h(n)** is the estimated cost to get from n to the goal.
- **f(n)** is the total estimated cost, which A* uses to prioritize the search.

A* algorithm works by exploring the nodes with the lowest **f(n)** value, ensuring the most promising paths are evaluated first.

*How A Works:**

1. Start by putting the starting node in an open list (nodes to be evaluated).
2. Evaluate the node with the lowest **f(n)** value.
3. For each neighbor of the current node:
   - If it's not in the open list, calculate its **f(n)** value and add it to the open list.
   - If it's already in the open list but the new path is better, update the **f(n)** value.

4. Repeat steps 2 and 3 until the goal is reached or the open list is empty.

A* guarantees an optimal solution if the heuristic function **h(n)** is admissible (i.e., it never overestimates the true cost).

Code Example (C++):

cpp

```cpp
#include <iostream>
#include <vector>
#include <queue>
#include <unordered_map>
#include <cmath>
using namespace std;

struct Node {
    int x, y;
    int g, h, f;
    Node* parent;

    Node(int x, int y) : x(x), y(y), g(0), h(0), f(0), parent(nullptr) {}
};

struct CompareNodes {
    bool operator()(Node* a, Node* b) {
        return a->f > b->f;
    }
};
```

```cpp
// Heuristic function: Manhattan distance
int heuristic(Node* a, Node* b) {
    return abs(a->x - b->x) + abs(a->y - b->y);
}


vector<Node*> AStarSearch(Node* start, Node* goal, int grid[5][5]) {
    priority_queue<Node*, vector<Node*>, CompareNodes> openList;
    unordered_map<int, unordered_map<int, Node*>> closedList;

    start->h = heuristic(start, goal);
    start->f = start->g + start->h;
    openList.push(start);

    vector<Node*> path;

    while (!openList.empty()) {
        Node* current = openList.top();
        openList.pop();

        // If goal is reached, reconstruct path
        if (current->x == goal->x && current->y == goal->y) {
            while (current != nullptr) {
                path.push_back(current);
                current = current->parent;
            }
            reverse(path.begin(), path.end());
            break;
        }
```

```
    // Check neighbors
    vector<pair<int, int>> neighbors = {{0, 1}, {1, 0}, {0, -1}, {-1, 0}};
    for (auto& neighbor : neighbors) {
        int nx = current->x + neighbor.first;
        int ny = current->y + neighbor.second;

        if (nx >= 0 && nx < 5 && ny >= 0 && ny < 5 && grid[nx][ny] == 0) {
            Node* neighborNode = new Node(nx, ny);
            neighborNode->g = current->g + 1;
            neighborNode->h = heuristic(neighborNode, goal);
            neighborNode->f = neighborNode->g + neighborNode->h;
            neighborNode->parent = current;

            // If the node is not in the closed list or if we found a better path
            if   (closedList[nx][ny]   ==   nullptr   ||   neighborNode->f   <
closedList[nx][ny]->f) {
                closedList[nx][ny] = neighborNode;
                openList.push(neighborNode);
            }
        }
    }
  }

  return path;
}

int main() {
  int grid[5][5] = {{0, 0, 1, 0, 0},
          {0, 0, 1, 0, 0},
          {0, 0, 0, 1, 0},
```

```
                {0, 1, 0, 0, 0},
                {0, 0, 0, 0, 0}};
    Node* start = new Node(0, 0);
    Node* goal = new Node(4, 4);


    vector<Node*> path = AStarSearch(start, goal, grid);
    for (Node* node : path) {
        cout << "(" << node->x << "," << node->y << ") ";
    }
    cout << endl;


    return 0;
}
```

Bidirectional Search

Bidirectional Search is an optimization of the standard search algorithms like BFS or DFS. It works by performing two simultaneous searches:

1. One from the start node toward the goal.
2. One from the goal node toward the start.

Both searches proceed until they meet in the middle. This drastically reduces the search space because instead of searching from the start to the goal in one direction, we search from both ends simultaneously.

- **Time Complexity**: In theory, bidirectional search can cut the search time by half, as the search space is effectively reduced to N\sqrt{N}N instead of NNN in a single-direction search.

However, bidirectional search is only applicable when there is a known and unambiguous path from the start to the goal.

Real-World Example: **Routing in navigation systems** — Bidirectional search can be used to find the shortest path between two points on a map by simultaneously searching from both the start and destination.

---

*IDA (Iterative Deepening A)***

IDA (Iterative Deepening A)** is an optimization that combines the best features of **depth-first search** (DFS) and **A***. It performs a **depth-first search** but limits the depth of the search to a certain threshold. If the threshold is exceeded, the search restarts with a higher threshold, progressively exploring deeper levels of the search space.

IDA* is particularly useful for large search spaces where memory is limited, as it only stores a single path in memory at a time, making it memory-efficient compared to A*.

- **Time Complexity**: The time complexity of IDA* is similar to A* but with the advantage of lower memory usage. It can be especially beneficial in large problem spaces where traditional A* might not be feasible.

Real-World Example: **Puzzle games** like **Sliding Puzzle** or **8-Puzzle** — where IDA* can efficiently find the solution by iteratively increasing the search depth without storing the entire search space.

Real-World Example: Solving the Shortest Path in a Map-Based Game

Imagine you are designing a **map-based game**, where a player needs to navigate from one point to another on a grid. The game has obstacles (walls) that prevent movement, and the goal is to find the shortest path from the player's starting position to the destination.

- **A***: You could use the A* algorithm to efficiently compute the shortest path considering obstacles.
- **Bidirectional Search**: If the map is large, you could apply bidirectional search to speed up the process by searching from both the start and the destination.
- **IDA***: For memory efficiency, you could use IDA* to solve the problem when dealing with very large maps.

For example, in a large open-world game with dynamic environments, you can apply A* to find the shortest path between the player and an objective. However, if the player is traversing through a series of regions and the goal is not fixed, bidirectional search can help reduce time complexity by searching from both ends. Alternatively, in a mobile game with limited memory, IDA* can provide an optimal solution with minimal memory overhead.

Advanced search algorithms like **A***, **Bidirectional Search**, and **IDA*** offer powerful ways to solve pathfinding problems efficiently. They are commonly used in AI, game development, robotics, and routing systems to navigate through large search spaces while optimizing performance. By understanding these algorithms and their real-world applications, you can select the most

Chapter 18: Computational Complexity and NP-Completeness

In this chapter, we will delve into **computational complexity** and explore the critical class of problems known as **NP-complete problems**. We will cover the fundamental concepts of how we measure the efficiency of algorithms and the challenges associated with solving certain complex problems. Finally, we will apply these concepts to real-world problems such as the **Traveling Salesman Problem (TSP)** and understand its computational limitations.

What is Computational Complexity?

Computational complexity is a field of computer science that studies the efficiency of algorithms, primarily focusing on the amount of resources they consume, such as **time** and **memory**. Understanding computational complexity is essential for analyzing how algorithms perform, especially when working with large datasets or solving computationally expensive problems.

There are two primary types of computational complexity:

1. **Time Complexity**: This measures the amount of time an algorithm takes to complete as a function of the input size.

It is often expressed in Big-O notation, which describes the upper bound of an algorithm's growth rate.

- For example, an algorithm with **O(n)** time complexity means that the time to execute the algorithm increases linearly with the input size.

2. **Space Complexity**: This measures the amount of memory an algorithm uses relative to the size of the input. Like time complexity, it is also expressed in Big-O notation.

   - For example, **O(n)** space complexity indicates that the memory usage increases linearly with the size of the input.

To evaluate an algorithm's efficiency, we look at its **worst-case**, **best-case**, and **average-case** complexities. The **worst-case complexity** is often the most important metric, as it provides an upper bound on the time or space the algorithm will require.

NP-Complete Problems and Their Significance

NP-complete problems form a critical class of problems in computational theory. To understand this concept, we need to first define two key classes of problems:

1. **P (Polynomial Time)**: This class consists of problems that can be solved in polynomial time, meaning that the time required to solve the problem grows at a manageable rate

(e.g., $O(n^2)$, $O(n^3)$). These problems are considered **efficiently solvable**.

2. **NP (Nondeterministic Polynomial Time)**: These are problems for which a proposed solution can be verified in polynomial time. In other words, given a solution, we can quickly check whether it's correct or not. However, finding the solution might take longer, and we don't know if there's a polynomial-time algorithm to solve the problem.

NP-complete problems are a subset of NP problems that are both:

1. **NP-hard**: These problems are at least as difficult as the hardest problems in NP.
2. **In NP**: These problems can be verified in polynomial time.

The **significance** of NP-complete problems lies in the fact that if we can find a polynomial-time algorithm for any NP-complete problem, it would imply that $P = NP$, meaning every NP problem could be solved in polynomial time. However, this is still an unsolved question in computer science, and most experts believe that $P \neq NP$. This implies that NP-complete problems are intrinsically difficult to solve.

Famous NP-Complete Problems:

- **Traveling Salesman Problem (TSP)**
- **Knapsack Problem**

- **Boolean Satisfiability Problem (SAT)**
- **Graph Coloring Problem**
- **Clique Problem**

Real-World Example: Solving the Traveling Salesman Problem (TSP) and Understanding Its Limitations

The **Traveling Salesman Problem (TSP)** is one of the most famous NP-complete problems. In this problem, a salesman needs to visit a set of cities exactly once and return to the starting city while minimizing the total travel distance. Despite its simple description, TSP is computationally hard to solve, especially as the number of cities increases.

Why TSP is NP-Complete:

- **Verification**: If you're given a specific route, it's easy to verify whether it visits every city once and calculates the total distance. This verification can be done in polynomial time.
- **Finding the Optimal Path**: However, finding the optimal path that minimizes the distance requires checking every possible combination of routes, which grows exponentially with the number of cities.

For example, if there are n cities, there are (n-1)! possible routes to evaluate. For small numbers of cities (e.g., 5 or 6), we can exhaustively compute all possible routes, but as n grows, the number of routes grows very quickly. For 20 cities, there are over 2.4 million possible routes, and for 100 cities, this number reaches astronomical levels.

Approximation Algorithms for TSP:

Since solving TSP optimally for large numbers of cities is computationally infeasible, we rely on **approximation algorithms** that provide near-optimal solutions in reasonable time. Some of the well-known approximation algorithms include:

1. **Nearest Neighbor Algorithm**: Start at any city, visit the nearest unvisited city, and continue until all cities have been visited.

    o This algorithm doesn't guarantee the optimal solution but provides a good solution in a short amount of time.

2. **Christofides' Algorithm**: This is an approximation algorithm for the metric TSP that guarantees a solution within 1.5 times the optimal solution. It works by combining minimum spanning trees and perfect matching.

3. **Genetic Algorithms and Simulated Annealing**: These are heuristic methods that use iterative processes to "evolve" toward an optimal or near-optimal solution. While these

algorithms do not guarantee an optimal solution, they often provide good results in practice for large instances.

Code Example: Solving a Small Instance of TSP (Brute Force)

cpp

```cpp
#include <iostream>
#include <vector>
#include <limits.h>
#include <algorithm>

using namespace std;

int calculateDistance(const vector<vector<int>>& dist, const vector<int>& path) {
    int totalDistance = 0;
    for (int i = 0; i < path.size() - 1; ++i) {
        totalDistance += dist[path[i]][path[i + 1]];
    }
    totalDistance += dist[path.back()][path[0]]; // Return to the start
    return totalDistance;
}

int tspBruteForce(const vector<vector<int>>& dist) {
    int n = dist.size();
    vector<int> cities(n);
    for (int i = 0; i < n; ++i) cities[i] = i;

    int minDistance = INT_MAX;
```

```
do {
    int currDistance = calculateDistance(dist, cities);
    minDistance = min(minDistance, currDistance);
} while (next_permutation(cities.begin(), cities.end()));   // Generate all permutations

    return minDistance;
}

int main() {
    vector<vector<int>> dist = {{0, 10, 15, 20},
                    {10, 0, 35, 25},
                    {15, 35, 0, 30},
                    {20, 25, 30, 0}};

    cout << "Minimum tour distance: " << tspBruteForce(dist) << endl;
    return 0;
}
```

In the code above, the function tspBruteForce calculates the minimum tour distance for a given distance matrix using brute-force. The next_permutation function generates all possible routes and calculates the total distance, keeping track of the minimum distance encountered.

Limitations and Insights:

While the brute-force method works for small instances (e.g., 4 cities in the example), it becomes impractical for larger numbers of cities due to the factorial growth of possible routes. This highlights the limitations of solving NP-complete problems like TSP exactly.

As the number of cities increases, even more sophisticated algorithms like **branch-and-bound** or **dynamic programming** might not provide feasible solutions within a reasonable amount of time for large inputs.

Understanding **computational complexity** and **NP-completeness** is crucial for tackling real-world problems in computer science. While **P** problems can be solved efficiently, **NP-complete** problems like TSP highlight the inherent difficulty of finding optimal solutions in complex domains. For many practical problems, we rely on approximation or heuristic algorithms to find solutions that are close to optimal, but that can be computed efficiently. This chapter provides a foundation for understanding how computational complexity impacts the design of algorithms and the trade-offs between exact solutions and practical feasibility.

Chapter 19: Randomized Algorithms

In this chapter, we will explore **randomized algorithms**, a powerful class of algorithms that leverage randomization to solve problems efficiently. These algorithms use random decisions to improve performance, especially when dealing with complex or large datasets. We will look at the role of randomness in algorithm design, examine key examples such as **randomized quicksort** and **Monte Carlo methods**, and provide a real-world example of how **random sampling** can be used in large datasets for approximations.

The Role of Randomness in Algorithms

Randomized algorithms are algorithms that make use of random numbers or random choices in their logic. These algorithms often provide significant improvements in performance, simplicity, or both, when compared to deterministic algorithms. While deterministic algorithms follow a fixed, predictable set of rules to solve a problem, randomized algorithms may produce different outputs each time they are run, depending on the random choices they make.

Randomized algorithms are typically used when:

1. **Performance is important**: Randomization can often speed up an algorithm or reduce its space requirements. For example, some randomized algorithms have **expected time complexities** that are better than their deterministic counterparts.

2. **Exactness is not always necessary**: In some cases, a near-correct solution is acceptable, and randomization can be used to approximate solutions to problems more efficiently.

3. **Problem complexity is high**: For certain complex problems, randomized algorithms can provide a practical way to explore solution spaces that would otherwise be infeasible for deterministic methods.

Types of Randomized Algorithms

There are two main types of randomized algorithms:

1. **Las Vegas Algorithms**: These algorithms always produce the correct result, but their running time depends on the random choices they make. The expected time complexity is generally better than that of a deterministic algorithm, but there is no guarantee about the worst-case performance.

2. **Monte Carlo Algorithms**: These algorithms may not always produce the correct result, but they provide a correct answer with a high probability. The running time is typically fixed and known in advance, but there is a small chance of error.

Examples of Randomized Algorithms

Randomized Quicksort

Quicksort is a well-known sorting algorithm that works by selecting a pivot element, partitioning the array around the pivot, and recursively sorting the subarrays. The efficiency of quicksort depends heavily on the choice of the pivot. In its deterministic version, quicksort always selects a fixed pivot (e.g., the first element, the last element, or the middle element).

Randomized Quicksort, on the other hand, improves the performance of quicksort by selecting the pivot element randomly. This ensures that the pivot is less likely to be poorly chosen, as it avoids the worst-case scenario where the pivot always ends up being the smallest or largest element in the array.

The expected time complexity of randomized quicksort is **O(n log n)**, which is much better than the deterministic quicksort's worst-case time complexity of **O(n²)**.

Code Example: Randomized Quicksort

cpp

```
#include <iostream>
#include <vector>
#include <cstdlib>
```

```cpp
#include <ctime>

using namespace std;

int partition(vector<int>& arr, int low, int high) {
    int pivot = arr[high];
    int i = low - 1;
    for (int j = low; j < high; j++) {
        if (arr[j] < pivot) {
            i++;
            swap(arr[i], arr[j]);
        }
    }
    swap(arr[i + 1], arr[high]);
    return i + 1;
}

int randomizedPartition(vector<int>& arr, int low, int high) {
    int pivotIndex = low + rand() % (high - low + 1);
    swap(arr[pivotIndex], arr[high]);
    return partition(arr, low, high);
}

void randomizedQuicksort(vector<int>& arr, int low, int high) {
    if (low < high) {
        int pi = randomizedPartition(arr, low, high);
        randomizedQuicksort(arr, low, pi - 1);
        randomizedQuicksort(arr, pi + 1, high);
    }
}
```

```
int main() {
    srand(time(0)); // Initialize random number generator
    vector<int> arr = {10, 80, 30, 90, 40, 50, 70};

    randomizedQuicksort(arr, 0, arr.size() - 1);

    cout << "Sorted array: ";
    for (int num : arr) {
        cout << num << " ";
    }
    cout << endl;

    return 0;
}
```

In this code, randomizedPartition randomly selects a pivot index before calling the regular partition function. This introduces randomness into the quicksort algorithm and helps prevent worst-case performance.

Monte Carlo Methods

Monte Carlo methods refer to a class of algorithms that rely on repeated random sampling to obtain numerical results. These methods are particularly useful when dealing with complex problems that have no deterministic solution or when an approximation is sufficient. Monte Carlo methods are widely used in fields such as **statistics, optimization, physics**, and **finance**.

For example, Monte Carlo methods can be used to estimate **pi** by randomly sampling points within a square and counting how many fall inside a circle. The ratio of the points inside the circle to the total points can be used to approximate the value of pi.

Code Example: Estimating Pi using Monte Carlo Method

cpp

```cpp
#include <iostream>
#include <cstdlib>
#include <ctime>
#include <cmath>

using namespace std;

double estimatePi(int numSamples) {
    int insideCircle = 0;

    for (int i = 0; i < numSamples; ++i) {
        double x = (double)rand() / RAND_MAX;
        double y = (double)rand() / RAND_MAX;

        if (x * x + y * y <= 1) {
            insideCircle++;
        }
    }

    return 4.0 * insideCircle / numSamples;
}
```

```
int main() {
    srand(time(0)); // Initialize random number generator

    int numSamples = 1000000;
    double piEstimate = estimatePi(numSamples);

    cout << "Estimated value of Pi: " << piEstimate << endl;

    return 0;
}
```

In this example, estimatePi uses random sampling to estimate the value of pi. The more samples you take, the more accurate the estimation becomes. This Monte Carlo method provides a way to approximate solutions to problems that would be too difficult or time-consuming to solve deterministically.

Real-World Example: Random Sampling in Large Datasets for Approximations

In real-world scenarios, especially when working with **big data**, it is often impractical or computationally expensive to analyze the entire dataset. **Random sampling** is a technique that allows you to select a subset of the data randomly and use this subset to estimate the properties of the entire dataset.

For example, in a large database of customer transactions, you might use random sampling to estimate the average purchase amount or the distribution of transaction types. By selecting a random sample of transactions, you can get a good approximation without needing to process every single transaction, which would be time-consuming.

A popular application of random sampling in data analysis is in **data sketching** techniques, such as **reservoir sampling**, which allows you to maintain a representative sample of data without knowing the total size of the dataset upfront.

Randomized algorithms offer a flexible and efficient approach to solving a wide range of problems, from sorting and searching to optimization and approximation. By incorporating randomness into algorithm design, these methods can improve performance, simplify implementation, and provide practical solutions to complex computational challenges. Whether using **randomized quicksort** for efficient sorting, **Monte Carlo methods** for probabilistic simulations, or **random sampling** for large-scale data analysis, randomized algorithms are a valuable tool in any programmer's toolkit.

Chapter 20: Parallel Algorithms

In this chapter, we will explore **parallel algorithms**, a powerful class of algorithms designed to take advantage of parallel computing environments. These algorithms can significantly improve performance by splitting a task into smaller sub-tasks that can be executed simultaneously. Parallel computing leverages multiple processors or cores to execute tasks concurrently, enabling faster problem-solving for computationally intensive problems. We will discuss the principles behind parallel computing, techniques for parallelizing algorithms, and provide a real-world example of **parallel matrix multiplication** to handle large datasets.

Introduction to Parallel Computing

Parallel computing is the simultaneous execution of multiple tasks (or threads) to solve a problem more efficiently. By breaking a large problem into smaller sub-problems and solving them concurrently, parallel algorithms exploit the full potential of multi-core processors or distributed computing systems.

Key concepts in parallel computing:

1. **Parallelism**: The concept of performing multiple computations at the same time. This is essential for

speeding up tasks like processing large datasets, performing simulations, or solving complex mathematical problems.

2. **Concurrency vs. Parallelism**: While concurrency refers to managing multiple tasks in an overlapping time frame (not necessarily simultaneously), parallelism involves executing multiple tasks simultaneously. In the context of parallel algorithms, parallelism refers to breaking down problems into smaller tasks that can run at the same time.

3. **Multi-core Processors**: Modern CPUs are designed with multiple cores, which allow the execution of multiple threads simultaneously. Parallel algorithms are designed to take advantage of these cores to speed up computations.

4. **Distributed Computing**: In large-scale computing, parallelism is achieved by distributing tasks across multiple machines in a network (e.g., cloud computing or high-performance computing clusters).

Techniques for Parallelizing Algorithms

Parallelizing algorithms involves breaking down a task into smaller sub-tasks that can be executed concurrently. Here are some techniques for parallelizing algorithms:

1. **Divide and Conquer**:

- o This technique breaks a problem into smaller sub-problems, solves each sub-problem independently, and combines their solutions.
- o Example: **Merge sort** and **quicksort** can be parallelized by sorting sub-arrays concurrently.

2. **Data Parallelism**:
   - o This technique involves performing the same operation on multiple pieces of data in parallel.
   - o Example: Adding the elements of two large arrays concurrently or processing pixels in an image simultaneously.

3. **Task Parallelism**:
   - o In task parallelism, different tasks (or threads) perform independent operations simultaneously, even if they operate on different data sets.
   - o Example: In a web server, one thread can handle incoming requests, while another processes requests for different users.

4. **Pipeline Parallelism**:
   - o This technique involves breaking a task into a sequence of stages, where each stage is executed concurrently.
   - o Example: In video processing, different stages like decoding, filtering, and encoding can be run in parallel.

5. **Fork-Join Model**:

- o This model divides a task into multiple subtasks (fork) and later combines the results (join). This model is commonly used in recursive algorithms.
- o Example: Parallelizing the calculation of a Fibonacci sequence where each recursive call can run in parallel.

Real-World Example: Parallel Matrix Multiplication for Large Datasets

Matrix multiplication is a fundamental operation in many scientific, engineering, and data-driven applications, such as computer graphics, machine learning, and simulations. For large datasets, matrix multiplication can be very computationally expensive, and parallelizing this operation can lead to significant performance gains.

Matrix Multiplication

Matrix multiplication involves multiplying two matrices AAA and BBB to produce a resulting matrix CCC. The formula for the element at position C[i][j]C[i][j]C[i][j] is given by:

C[i][j]=∑k=1nA[i][k]×B[k][j]C[i][j] = \sum_{k=1}^{n} A[i][k] \times B[k][j]C[i][j]=k=1∑nA[i][k]×B[k][j]

For large matrices, this calculation can become very time-consuming. By parallelizing the computation, we can significantly speed up the process by calculating multiple elements of matrix CCC simultaneously.

Parallel Matrix Multiplication: Strategy

1. **Data Parallelism**:
   - Matrix multiplication is highly parallelizable because each element C[i][j]C[i][j]C[i][j] can be computed independently of the others.
   - Each row of matrix AAA can be multiplied with each column of matrix BBB concurrently.

2. **Row/Column Decomposition**:
   - **Row decomposition**: Divide the rows of matrix AAA into chunks, and assign each chunk to a different processor.
   - **Column decomposition**: Similarly, divide the columns of matrix BBB and assign chunks to processors.

3. **MapReduce**:
   - MapReduce can be used to handle matrix multiplication by distributing matrix elements to different nodes and using the reduce phase to compute partial results and combine them.

Code Example: Parallel Matrix Multiplication in C++

Here is an example of **parallel matrix multiplication** using OpenMP, a popular parallel programming library:

cpp

```cpp
#include <iostream>
#include <vector>
#include <omp.h> // OpenMP library for parallel programming

using namespace std;

void parallelMatrixMultiply(const vector<vector<int>>& A, const vector<vector<int>>& B, vector<vector<int>>& C, int n) {
    #pragma omp parallel for collapse(2) // Parallelize nested loops
    for (int i = 0; i < n; ++i) {
        for (int j = 0; j < n; ++j) {
            C[i][j] = 0;
            for (int k = 0; k < n; ++k) {
                C[i][j] += A[i][k] * B[k][j];
            }
        }
    }
}

int main() {
    int n = 4; // Size of the matrix
    vector<vector<int>> A(n, vector<int>(n, 1)); // Matrix A (4x4) filled with 1s
    vector<vector<int>> B(n, vector<int>(n, 2)); // Matrix B (4x4) filled with 2s
    vector<vector<int>> C(n, vector<int>(n, 0)); // Result matrix C (4x4)
```

```
// Set the number of threads for OpenMP
omp_set_num_threads(4);

parallelMatrixMultiply(A, B, C, n);

// Print the resulting matrix C
cout << "Matrix C (Result):\n";
for (int i = 0; i < n; ++i) {
    for (int j = 0; j < n; ++j) {
        cout << C[i][j] << " ";
    }
    cout << endl;
}

    return 0;
}
```

In this code:

- **OpenMP** directives (#pragma omp parallel for collapse(2)) are used to parallelize the nested loops responsible for matrix multiplication.
- Each thread computes different elements of the result matrix **C** simultaneously.

Performance Improvement

By running the matrix multiplication on multiple threads, we can significantly reduce the computation time for large matrices. For example, a matrix multiplication that would take several seconds to complete on a single processor might only take a fraction of a second on multiple processors. This speedup is especially noticeable with matrices of size 1000×10001000 \times 10001000×1000 or larger.

Parallel algorithms harness the power of multi-core processors and distributed computing systems to solve problems faster and more efficiently. By breaking down complex tasks into smaller, independent subtasks, parallel algorithms enable us to handle computationally expensive operations like matrix multiplication, graph traversal, and sorting on large datasets. Understanding how to design and implement parallel algorithms is essential for optimizing performance in fields such as data science, scientific computing, and machine learning.

Chapter 21: Machine Learning Algorithms

In this chapter, we will explore **machine learning (ML) algorithms**, which are fundamental to modern data analysis and AI-driven applications. Machine learning algorithms allow computers to learn from data, identify patterns, and make decisions or predictions without being explicitly programmed. We will cover key machine learning algorithms, such as **linear regression**, **k-means clustering**, and **decision trees**, and provide a real-world example of how to implement a simple machine learning algorithm in **C++**.

Overview of Machine Learning and Its Algorithmic Foundations

Machine learning is a subset of artificial intelligence (AI) that focuses on building systems that can learn from data, improve performance, and make decisions without human intervention. The core idea behind machine learning is that algorithms can automatically identify patterns in data, generalize from examples, and make predictions or classifications.

There are three main types of machine learning:

1. **Supervised Learning**:

- The algorithm is trained on labeled data, where both input and output are provided.
- Example algorithms: Linear regression, decision trees, support vector machines.

2. **Unsupervised Learning**:
   - The algorithm is trained on unlabeled data, and the system tries to identify patterns or structures within the data.
   - Example algorithms: K-means clustering, hierarchical clustering, principal component analysis (PCA).

3. **Reinforcement Learning**:
   - The algorithm learns by interacting with an environment and receiving feedback in the form of rewards or punishments.
   - Example: Q-learning, deep Q-networks (DQN).

In this chapter, we will focus on supervised and unsupervised learning algorithms, which are the most commonly used in practical machine learning applications.

Key Algorithms

1. **Linear Regression**

Linear regression is one of the simplest machine learning algorithms used for predicting a continuous output based on one or more input features. It establishes a linear relationship between the input variables (independent variables) and the output (dependent variable).

The equation for simple linear regression is:

$y=mx+b$ y $= mx + b$ y$=mx+b$

Where:

- yyy is the predicted output (dependent variable).
- mmm is the slope of the line (coefficient).
- xxx is the input feature (independent variable).
- bbb is the y-intercept (bias).

In multiple linear regression, the model uses more than one input feature to predict the output.

Application of Linear Regression:

Linear regression can be used in areas such as:

- Predicting house prices based on features like size, location, and age.
- Estimating the cost of production based on material costs and labor hours.

2. K-Means Clustering

K-means is an **unsupervised learning** algorithm used for clustering, where the goal is to group similar data points into clusters based on their features. The algorithm iteratively assigns data points to clusters and then re-calculates the centroids (the center of each cluster) until convergence.

The steps of the K-means algorithm are:

1. **Initialize**: Choose K initial centroids (either randomly or using heuristics).
2. **Assign**: Assign each data point to the nearest centroid.
3. **Update**: Recalculate the centroids of the clusters by averaging the points assigned to each centroid.
4. **Repeat**: Repeat the assign-update steps until the centroids do not change significantly or a maximum number of iterations is reached.

Application of K-Means:

K-means is widely used in applications such as:

- Customer segmentation for targeted marketing.
- Image compression by clustering similar pixels.
- Anomaly detection by identifying outliers that do not belong to any cluster.

3. Decision Trees

A **decision tree** is a tree-like structure used for both classification and regression tasks. Each internal node of the tree represents a decision based on a feature, and each leaf node represents the outcome or prediction. The algorithm recursively splits the data into subsets based on the feature values that best separate the data.

The construction of a decision tree involves choosing the feature that maximizes the **information gain** (for classification) or **variance reduction** (for regression) at each split. This process continues until a stopping criterion is met, such as a minimum number of data points in a node or a maximum tree depth.

Application of Decision Trees:
Decision trees are used in:

- Predicting loan approval based on customer attributes (income, age, credit score).
- Classifying emails as spam or not based on various features (subject line, sender, content).
- Medical diagnosis by classifying patients into different risk categories.

Real-World Example: Implementing a Simple Machine Learning Algorithm in C++

To bring these concepts into practice, let's implement a **simple linear regression** algorithm in **C++**. This example demonstrates how machine learning models can be implemented from scratch, showcasing both the theoretical aspects of linear regression and the application of algorithms in code.

Linear Regression Implementation in C++

Here is an example of how to implement a simple linear regression algorithm in C++ to predict a value based on input data:

cpp

```cpp
#include <iostream>
#include <vector>
#include <numeric>

using namespace std;

// Function to calculate the mean of a vector of numbers
double mean(const vector<double>& v) {
    return accumulate(v.begin(), v.end(), 0.0) / v.size();
}

// Function to calculate the coefficients of linear regression (slope and intercept)
pair<double, double> linearRegression(const vector<double>& X, const vector<double>& Y) {
    double x_mean = mean(X);
```

```
    double y_mean = mean(Y);
    double numerator = 0.0;
    double denominator = 0.0;

    for (size_t i = 0; i < X.size(); ++i) {
        numerator += (X[i] - x_mean) * (Y[i] - y_mean);
        denominator += (X[i] - x_mean) * (X[i] - x_mean);
    }

    double slope = numerator / denominator;
    double intercept = y_mean - (slope * x_mean);
    return {slope, intercept};
}

int main() {
    // Sample data points
    vector<double> X = {1, 2, 3, 4, 5}; // Independent variable (e.g., years of experience)
    vector<double> Y = {1, 2, 1.3, 3.75, 2.25}; // Dependent variable (e.g., salary)

    // Get the linear regression coefficients
    pair<double, double> coefficients = linearRegression(X, Y);
    double slope = coefficients.first;
    double intercept = coefficients.second;

    // Display the result: y = mx + b
    cout << "Linear regression equation: y = " << slope << "x + " << intercept << endl;
```

```
// Predict a value
double prediction = slope * 6 + intercept; // Predict for X = 6
cout << "Predicted value for X = 6: " << prediction << endl;

    return 0;
}
```

Explanation of the Code:

- The **mean()** function calculates the average value of a dataset.

- The **linearRegression()** function calculates the slope and intercept of the linear regression line using the **least squares** method.

- In the **main()** function, we input the data for **X** (independent variable) and **Y** (dependent variable), calculate the regression coefficients, and then predict the value for an unknown input.

Example Output:

yaml

Linear regression equation: y = 0.65x + 0.25
Predicted value for X = 6: 4.15

In this example, the **slope** is 0.65, and the **intercept** is 0.25, forming the equation y=0.65x+0.25y = 0.65x + 0.25y=0.65x+0.25. Given an input of X=6X = 6X=6, the predicted value for YYY is 4.15.

Machine learning algorithms provide powerful tools for analyzing data, making predictions, and solving complex problems. In this chapter, we covered some of the fundamental algorithms, including **linear regression**, **k-means clustering**, and **decision trees**. Each algorithm has its own strengths and applications, and understanding their foundations is key to implementing them effectively in real-world scenarios.

We also demonstrated how to implement a simple machine learning algorithm (linear regression) in **C++**, showing the practical steps involved in creating machine learning models from scratch. While this example is simple, it lays the groundwork for understanding more complex algorithms and their applications in data science and AI.

Chapter 22: Final Thoughts and Future Trends in Algorithm Design

In this final chapter, we will explore the **future of algorithm design** and the emerging trends that will define the next generation of computational technologies. Algorithms are at the heart of all modern computing, from mobile apps and web services to machine learning and AI-driven systems. As technology continues to advance, new challenges arise that demand innovative solutions and more efficient algorithms. Understanding these trends and developments will be crucial for anyone interested in the future of computer science and software engineering.

Emerging Trends in Algorithm Design and Development

The landscape of algorithm design is continually evolving. While classical algorithms still form the foundation of many applications, new challenges, and opportunities are driving the development of **novel algorithms** in various domains. Some of the key emerging trends include:

1. **Algorithms for Big Data**:
   o The explosion of data in various fields, such as social media, healthcare, finance, and e-commerce,

has led to the need for algorithms that can process and analyze **massive datasets** efficiently.

- o Traditional algorithms often struggle with the scale of big data. As a result, algorithms for **distributed computing** and **parallel processing** have become increasingly important.

- o **MapReduce**, **Apache Hadoop**, and **Spark** are examples of tools and frameworks designed to process big data by breaking down tasks into smaller, manageable units that can be executed in parallel across multiple machines.

2. **Machine Learning and AI Algorithms**:

- o As machine learning and artificial intelligence (AI) continue to gain traction, there is a growing need for algorithms that can handle complex tasks such as pattern recognition, optimization, and decision-making.

- o Deep learning algorithms, which model the brain's neural networks, are at the forefront of AI research and have revolutionized fields such as image and speech recognition, natural language processing, and robotics.

- o Innovations in **reinforcement learning**, **transfer learning**, and **meta-learning** are expected to lead to more adaptable and intelligent systems that can learn from fewer examples and generalize across a variety of tasks.

3. **Quantum Computing Algorithms**:

   o Quantum computing has the potential to revolutionize algorithm design. **Quantum algorithms** exploit the principles of quantum mechanics to solve problems that would be infeasible for classical computers to handle.

   o Quantum computers leverage phenomena like **superposition** and **entanglement** to perform calculations in parallel, potentially speeding up tasks such as cryptography, optimization, and machine learning.

   o Notable algorithms, such as **Shor's algorithm** (for factoring large numbers) and **Grover's algorithm** (for searching unsorted databases), show that quantum computers could outperform classical computers in specific domains.

   o As quantum computing hardware continues to improve, algorithm designers will need to adapt their methods to fully harness the power of these systems.

4. **Approximation and Heuristic Algorithms**:

   o As the complexity of problems increases, exact solutions often become computationally expensive

MASTERING ALGORITHMS WITH C++

or practically impossible to achieve. In these cases, **approximation algorithms** provide near-optimal solutions in a fraction of the time.

- o **Heuristic algorithms** such as **genetic algorithms**, **simulated annealing**, and **ant colony optimization** are gaining popularity for solving problems in optimization, scheduling, and machine learning.

- o These algorithms are particularly useful for problems where finding an exact solution would take too long or is not feasible within the required constraints.

5. **Algorithmic Fairness and Ethics**:

- o With the increasing influence of algorithms in decision-making processes (e.g., credit scoring, hiring, law enforcement), concerns about **algorithmic fairness** and **bias** have risen.

- o There is growing interest in designing algorithms that not only optimize performance but also ensure fairness, transparency, and accountability. This includes developing methods to detect and mitigate bias in machine learning models and ensuring that algorithms are not inadvertently perpetuating social inequalities.

The Future of Algorithms in Big Data, AI, and Quantum Computing

The future of algorithms is closely tied to the continued advancements in **big data**, **artificial intelligence**, and **quantum computing**. These areas are set to become more intertwined, and understanding the algorithms driving these fields will be crucial for future technologists.

1. **Big Data and Algorithms**:
    o   As data continues to grow at an exponential rate, we will need **more efficient algorithms** to extract meaningful insights from massive datasets. Techniques like **real-time data processing**, **stream processing**, and **distributed machine learning** will become increasingly common in industries such as finance, healthcare, and marketing.
    o   **Data mining** algorithms will evolve to detect patterns and trends in unstructured data, such as text, audio, and video, which are becoming more prevalent in today's digital world.

2. **AI and Deep Learning**:
    o   The deep learning revolution shows no signs of slowing down. As neural networks become larger and more complex, new **training algorithms** and **optimization techniques** will emerge to handle increasingly intricate architectures.

- o AI will continue to shape fields such as natural language processing (e.g., chatbots and translation services), autonomous vehicles, and **predictive analytics**.

- o Algorithms for reinforcement learning will become more advanced, allowing machines to perform tasks autonomously, such as robotic manipulation, game-playing, and resource management.

3. **Quantum Computing Algorithms**:

- o **Quantum computing** holds the potential to solve problems that classical computers cannot tackle efficiently. For example, quantum computers could be used for complex **optimization problems**, cryptography, and simulations of molecular structures for drug discovery.

- o While practical, large-scale quantum computers are still in their infancy, the development of **quantum-safe algorithms** and **quantum algorithms** will likely be the key to unlocking the true potential of quantum computing.

- o We will likely see **quantum algorithm design** become a distinct area of focus, requiring deep knowledge of both quantum mechanics and traditional algorithm design.

Real-World Example: How Algorithmic Thinking Will Shape Future Technologies

One of the most exciting areas where algorithmic thinking will have a transformative impact is in **autonomous vehicles**. The development of self-driving cars relies on an array of algorithms working in tandem to process sensor data, navigate roads, and make real-time decisions.

For example, algorithms used in **pathfinding** (such as *A search**) allow autonomous cars to find the optimal route while avoiding obstacles, traffic, and construction zones. Machine learning algorithms help vehicles understand complex road environments, such as identifying pedestrians, cyclists, and other vehicles in real-time.

Additionally, quantum computing could revolutionize the optimization algorithms used for autonomous vehicles, allowing for faster decision-making and more efficient routing under unpredictable conditions, such as during a traffic jam or in highly congested urban areas.

This real-world example demonstrates how advancements in algorithm design will not only improve existing technologies but also give rise to entirely new systems that we once thought were science fiction.

As we've seen throughout this book, algorithms are the backbone of modern computing and will continue to evolve in exciting ways. The future of algorithm design is intertwined with advancements in big data, artificial intelligence, and quantum computing. As new challenges emerge, the development of innovative algorithms will be crucial for solving complex problems and pushing the boundaries of what is possible in computing.

Whether it's processing large datasets, powering autonomous systems, or harnessing the power of quantum computing, algorithmic thinking will play a central role in shaping future technologies. For aspiring computer scientists and software engineers, understanding these emerging trends and mastering algorithmic techniques will be key to staying ahead of the curve in a rapidly changing technological landscape.

www.ingramcontent.com/pod-product-compliance
Lightning Source LLC
LaVergne TN
LVHW022341060326
832902LV00022B/4176